System Hardening: A Comprehensive Guide to Securing Servers

James Relington

DEDICATION

To those who seek knowledge, inspiration, and new perspectives—
may this book be a companion on your journey, a spark for curiosity,
and a reminder that every page turned is a step toward discovery.

AKNOWLEDGEMENTS

I would like to express my deepest gratitude to everyone who contributed to the creation of this book. To my colleagues and mentors, your insights and expertise have been invaluable. A special thank you to my family and friends for their unwavering support and encouragement throughout this journey.

System Hardening Basics: Introduction to Securing Servers

In today's rapidly evolving digital landscape, securing servers has become a fundamental task for any organization that relies on technology. Servers play a crucial role in hosting applications, databases, and services that support business operations, making them prime targets for attackers. System hardening is the process of securing servers by reducing vulnerabilities and minimizing the attack surface. It involves applying various security measures and configurations to ensure that a server is protected from common threats, such as unauthorized access, data breaches, and service disruptions. As cyber threats become increasingly sophisticated, understanding the basics of system hardening is essential for safeguarding critical infrastructure.

The primary goal of system hardening is to enhance the security of a server by reducing the potential points of exploitation. Every server, whether it's a web server, database server, or file server, is susceptible to attacks if not properly secured. Attackers constantly seek to exploit weak spots in servers to gain unauthorized access, launch malware, or disrupt services. This is why hardening a system from the start is crucial in minimizing risks. By following a systematic approach to server hardening, organizations can prevent many common threats and reduce the chances of a successful attack.

One of the first steps in the hardening process is to perform a thorough assessment of the server's current security posture. This involves identifying potential vulnerabilities, misconfigurations, and weaknesses in the system that could be exploited by attackers. This assessment serves as a baseline for the hardening process and helps determine the necessary security measures to implement. It's also important to stay updated on the latest security patches and software updates, as attackers often target unpatched systems. Servers that are running outdated software or firmware are more likely to be vulnerable to attacks. Regularly applying security patches is an essential part of system hardening, as it addresses known vulnerabilities before they can be exploited.

One significant aspect of system hardening is reducing the server's attack surface by disabling unnecessary services and features. Servers often come with a variety of services and software pre-installed that may not be needed for the specific tasks the server is intended to perform. These unnecessary services increase the number of potential entry points for attackers. By disabling or removing services that are not required, administrators can significantly reduce the risk of an attack. For example, if a server is not being used to host a web application, the web server software should be disabled to prevent web-based attacks. Similarly, any unused ports or network services should be closed to further limit the server's exposure to the internet.

Another critical component of system hardening is configuring strong user access controls and permissions. Servers often have multiple users with different levels of access, and ensuring that each user has the appropriate permissions is crucial in preventing unauthorized actions. Administrators should follow the principle of least privilege, ensuring that each user has only the access necessary to perform their job functions. This reduces the likelihood of unauthorized access to sensitive information or critical system resources. Additionally, strong password policies should be enforced to prevent weak or easily guessed passwords from compromising the server's security. Passwords should be complex and changed regularly to reduce the chances of an account being hacked.

Securing network communication is also a vital part of system hardening. Servers often communicate with other devices over the network, and unprotected communication channels can expose sensitive data to interception and tampering. Using encryption protocols, such as Secure Socket Layer (SSL) or Transport Layer Security (TLS), ensures that data transmitted between the server and other devices remains confidential and secure. Additionally, securing remote access to the server is essential for preventing unauthorized users from gaining control over the system. Administrators should implement secure remote access methods, such as Virtual Private Networks (VPNs) or Secure Shell (SSH), to protect the integrity of the server and its data.

In addition to these technical measures, regular monitoring and auditing of the server's activities are essential for detecting potential security incidents. By continuously monitoring server logs and system events, administrators can identify suspicious behavior, such as unauthorized login attempts or abnormal network traffic patterns, that may indicate an ongoing attack. Intrusion detection and prevention systems (IDPS) can be implemented to automatically detect and respond to security threats in real-time. These systems analyze network traffic and server activity to identify potential security breaches and take action to mitigate the threat.

Backup and disaster recovery strategies are also an important aspect of system hardening. While hardening a server can greatly reduce the risk of an attack, no security measure can provide 100% protection. In the event of a successful attack or system failure, having a robust backup and recovery plan ensures that critical data can be restored and operations can resume quickly. Regular backups should be taken and stored securely, ideally offsite or in the cloud, to protect against data loss from hardware failures, malware, or ransomware attacks.

System hardening is an ongoing process that requires continuous attention and vigilance. As new vulnerabilities and threats emerge, administrators must stay informed about the latest security developments and apply patches, updates, and best practices to keep the server secure. Additionally, it is essential to regularly reassess the server's security posture and adjust the hardening measures as necessary. By maintaining a proactive approach to system hardening, organizations can better protect their servers against evolving threats and ensure the long-term security of their infrastructure.

In conclusion, system hardening is a critical process for securing servers and protecting them from common threats. It involves reducing vulnerabilities, minimizing the attack surface, implementing strong access controls, securing network communication, and continuously monitoring the system for potential threats. By following best practices for system hardening, organizations can ensure that their servers remain secure, reliable, and resilient in the face of evolving cyber threats.

The Importance of System Hardening in Modern IT Environments

In the contemporary landscape of information technology, system hardening has become an indispensable practice for ensuring the security and resilience of IT infrastructures. As organizations increasingly depend on digital systems for operations, the complexity of the environments they operate in grows. Servers, applications, databases, and networks must interact seamlessly to provide services, but this interconnectivity also opens doors for potential threats. With cyberattacks becoming more frequent and sophisticated, hardening systems is no longer a luxury; it is a necessity. The practice of system hardening is vital in securing servers and other critical infrastructure from the various and evolving threats they face.

The exponential growth of data and digital services has transformed the way businesses and organizations operate. Servers, which were once isolated and used for simple, internal purposes, are now often exposed to the wider internet. They host applications, store critical data, and facilitate communication across multiple systems. This increased exposure makes them more vulnerable to a wide range of cyber threats, including unauthorized access, data theft, denial of service attacks, and ransomware. The importance of system hardening in such an environment cannot be overstated. Hardening a system involves securing it by minimizing potential vulnerabilities and eliminating unnecessary services, ports, and configurations that attackers might exploit.

One of the primary reasons system hardening is critical in modern IT environments is the increased frequency and variety of cyberattacks. Cybercriminals are continuously evolving their tactics to exploit weaknesses in IT systems, often taking advantage of outdated software, unpatched vulnerabilities, or poorly configured security settings. In fact, many high-profile data breaches can be traced back to systems that were not adequately hardened or maintained. Hackers use various techniques, such as phishing, brute-force attacks, and malware, to infiltrate vulnerable systems and steal valuable information. In response to this ever-growing threat, organizations must adopt a proactive approach to system hardening. By applying rigorous security measures and best practices from the outset, IT teams can significantly reduce the risk of successful attacks.

Another reason system hardening is essential is the increased regulatory pressure on organizations to protect sensitive data. With laws such as the General Data Protection Regulation (GDPR) in Europe and the California Consumer Privacy Act (CCPA) in the United States, organizations are legally required to safeguard personal information and ensure the security of their systems. Failure to comply with these regulations can result in heavy fines and reputational damage. System hardening plays a pivotal role in meeting these regulatory requirements. For instance, implementing strong access controls, encryption, and regular patching helps to prevent unauthorized access to sensitive data, thereby ensuring compliance with data protection laws. Additionally, hardening measures such as logging and monitoring server activities allow organizations to detect and respond to security incidents quickly, which is often a legal requirement under such regulations.

The growing trend of remote work and the increasing use of cloud services further underline the importance of system hardening. As more employees access corporate resources from remote locations or cloud-based environments, the attack surface expands. Systems that were once securely contained within an organization's internal network are now exposed to potential threats from outside sources. Cloud services, while offering great flexibility and scalability, also present new security challenges. Data and applications hosted in the cloud are subject to different security risks than those on-premises. Therefore, securing servers, whether they are on-premises or hosted in the cloud, requires a robust and proactive approach to hardening. This includes implementing strong authentication mechanisms, encrypting data both at rest and in transit, and ensuring that cloud infrastructure is configured according to best security practices.

Moreover, as organizations increasingly rely on complex, interconnected systems, ensuring the security of each component becomes even more critical. A single vulnerability in one part of the system can potentially compromise the entire infrastructure. Hardening, in this context, involves not just securing individual servers but also ensuring that all systems within the IT environment are properly configured and protected. This includes securing network devices, endpoints, and user workstations, as well as ensuring that software and firmware are kept up to date with the latest security patches. Failure to harden any one of these components can provide attackers with an entry point, leading to a wider compromise of the organization's entire digital ecosystem.

The process of system hardening also contributes to the stability and performance of IT systems. Many security vulnerabilities arise from improper configurations or unpatched software, which can lead to system instability and decreased performance. By ensuring that systems are hardened, organizations not only mitigate security risks but also enhance the overall reliability and efficiency of their infrastructure. For example, eliminating unnecessary services reduces the resource consumption on a server, improving its speed and responsiveness. Additionally, by implementing security measures such as firewalls, intrusion detection systems, and secure network protocols, organizations can ensure that their servers remain operational and available, even in the face of potential threats.

A key aspect of system hardening is continuous monitoring and regular updates. The IT landscape is constantly evolving, with new vulnerabilities and threats emerging regularly. Hardening a system is not a one-time task but an ongoing process. This includes continuously monitoring the network for signs of unusual activity, applying security patches as soon as they are released, and reassessing the security posture of the system as new threats emerge. By keeping systems up to date and adjusting security protocols as needed, organizations can stay ahead of attackers and ensure their systems remain secure in an ever-changing threat landscape.

In modern IT environments, the significance of system hardening extends beyond mere protection against cyberattacks. It also enhances the organization's ability to respond to security incidents and ensures business continuity. By establishing a strong security foundation, hardening helps to minimize the potential damage caused by an attack and enables faster recovery. For instance, having a secure backup system in place ensures that critical data can be restored after an attack, minimizing downtime and loss of information. Additionally, hardening makes it more difficult for attackers to gain unauthorized access, making it less likely that a breach will lead to catastrophic consequences.

Given the increasing complexity and interconnectedness of modern IT environments, system hardening is more important than ever. As organizations continue to embrace digital transformation, they must recognize the critical role that system hardening plays in securing their infrastructure. By reducing vulnerabilities, applying security best practices, and continuously monitoring systems, organizations can protect themselves against the growing array of cyber threats they face daily. Hardening systems is not just a technical requirement but a strategic investment in the long-term security and success of the organization. It empowers businesses to operate confidently in an increasingly hostile digital world, safeguarding their assets, reputation, and future growth.

Identifying Common Threats to Servers

In today's interconnected world, servers are integral components of nearly every IT infrastructure. They store valuable data, host critical applications, and provide services that organizations rely on to operate smoothly. However, with this central role comes increased risk. Servers are prime targets for cybercriminals, and understanding the common threats that they face is essential for developing an effective security strategy. Identifying these threats is the first step in mitigating risks and safeguarding valuable resources. Servers are vulnerable to a variety of threats, each with its own set of attack vectors, and an awareness of these risks is fundamental to any robust defense.

One of the most common threats faced by servers is unauthorized access. Attackers constantly seek ways to gain unauthorized entry into systems to exploit sensitive data, install malware, or compromise network security. A successful intrusion can have devastating consequences, ranging from data theft to the complete disruption of services. Cybercriminals employ various tactics to gain unauthorized access, including brute-force attacks, where they attempt to guess or crack passwords by trying many different combinations until they find the correct one. Another method is exploiting weak or poorly configured access controls, such as default credentials that are not changed after installation. These weak points make it easier for attackers to gain entry and compromise the system.

In addition to unauthorized access, denial of service (DoS) attacks pose a significant threat to servers. A DoS attack involves overwhelming a server with excessive requests, which can lead to the server becoming slow or completely unavailable. Distributed denial of service (DDoS) attacks are an even more dangerous variant, where the attack is launched from multiple sources, making it difficult to stop. Servers that handle high volumes of traffic or offer essential services, such as web hosting or email, are particularly vulnerable to these attacks. A successful DDoS attack can cause significant downtime, leading to lost revenue, reputation damage, and increased operational costs. These types of attacks often target the availability of services rather than directly compromising the data on a server, but the disruption they cause can be equally damaging.

Malware is another prevalent threat to servers. Malicious software, including viruses, worms, ransomware, and Trojans, can infect a server and lead to various harmful outcomes. For instance, ransomware can encrypt server files and demand payment for the decryption key, locking organizations out of their own data. Other types of malware, such as worms, can spread across the network, infecting multiple devices and creating a larger attack surface. Trojans can be used to create backdoors in the server, giving attackers ongoing access to the system. These types of malware often exploit known vulnerabilities in the server's operating system or software applications. When malware is able to infiltrate a server, it can cause significant data loss, corruption, or theft, compromising the integrity of the server and the organization as a whole.

Another critical threat to servers is the exploitation of vulnerabilities within software and operating systems. Over time, developers discover flaws and weaknesses in their code, which can be exploited by attackers to gain control over a system. These vulnerabilities may exist in the server's operating system, web applications, or other software components running on the server. Attackers are often quick to target these weaknesses, especially when they are well-known and not patched. Unpatched software is one of the most common ways that systems are compromised. Regular patching and updates are essential to protecting servers from such vulnerabilities. When patches are ignored or delayed, the server becomes an easy target for exploitation, leaving the organization exposed to a variety of potential threats.

Social engineering attacks are also an emerging concern for server security. These attacks manipulate individuals into divulging sensitive information, often by impersonating trusted figures or exploiting human psychology. Phishing emails are a common example of social engineering, where attackers trick users into clicking on malicious links or providing login credentials. Once the attacker gains access to the server, they can use this information to escalate privileges or exfiltrate data. While these attacks may not exploit technical vulnerabilities directly, they can provide attackers with the means to bypass technical defenses, making them just as dangerous. Social engineering is increasingly being used in conjunction with other types of attacks, such as malware or ransomware, to gain initial access to a system.

Insider threats are also a significant risk to servers. These threats originate from individuals within the organization who have authorized access to the server, such as employees, contractors, or third-party vendors. Insiders can intentionally or unintentionally compromise server security by misusing their privileges. For example, an employee might inadvertently expose sensitive data or fail to follow security protocols, creating vulnerabilities that attackers can exploit. In other cases, an insider may intentionally sabotage the server or steal data for personal gain. Insider threats are particularly challenging to defend against, as they often bypass external security measures. Organizations must implement strict access controls, conduct regular audits, and educate employees about security best practices to minimize the risk of insider threats.

SQL injection attacks are another common and dangerous threat to web servers. In these attacks, the attacker inserts malicious SQL code into a web form or URL query, which the server processes as part of its database query. If the server is not properly sanitized, this code can manipulate the database, allowing the attacker to view or alter sensitive data. In some cases, attackers may use SQL injection to escalate their privileges or gain unauthorized access to the server. SQL injection vulnerabilities are common in web applications that fail to properly validate and sanitize user input. These attacks can have devastating consequences, particularly for servers that store critical data such as customer information, financial records, or intellectual property.

Cross-site scripting (XSS) is another type of vulnerability that primarily affects web servers. In an XSS attack, the attacker injects malicious scripts into web pages that are then executed in the browsers of users who visit the site. These scripts can be used to steal session cookies, redirect users to phishing sites, or infect their machines with malware. XSS attacks can be difficult to detect because they target client-side components rather than server-side vulnerabilities. Servers hosting web applications must implement proper input validation and content security policies to mitigate the risk of XSS attacks.

Finally, one of the most insidious threats to servers is the possibility of privilege escalation. In this type of attack, the attacker gains limited access to a server, typically through a vulnerability, and then escalates their privileges to gain full control over the system. Privilege escalation is often achieved through exploiting bugs in software or using stolen credentials. Once the attacker has escalated their privileges, they can execute arbitrary commands, install malicious software, or exfiltrate sensitive data. Privilege escalation is a dangerous attack because it allows the attacker to move from a limited user account to full administrative access, which opens the door to significant damage.

Understanding and identifying these common threats to servers is the first step in securing an organization's infrastructure. Once these threats are recognized, administrators can implement appropriate countermeasures to mitigate the risks and enhance the overall security of the server environment. From patching vulnerabilities to implementing strong access controls, every measure taken to address these threats strengthens the server's defenses and reduces the likelihood of a successful attack. Recognizing the evolving nature of these threats is crucial for staying ahead of cybercriminals and ensuring that servers remain protected in an increasingly hostile digital landscape.

Minimizing the Attack Surface: Reducing Unnecessary Services

In the world of server security, one of the most effective ways to reduce vulnerability is to minimize the attack surface. This concept refers to reducing the number of potential entry points that attackers could exploit to gain unauthorized access to a system. A critical part of minimizing the attack surface involves reducing unnecessary services, software, and open ports on a server. Servers are designed to handle a wide variety of tasks, but often, they are configured with a broad range of services that are not required for the specific functions they need to perform. These unnecessary services introduce additional points of potential attack, making it easier for attackers to exploit vulnerabilities and compromise the system. By carefully evaluating and limiting the services running on a server, administrators can greatly enhance security and reduce the risk of attack.

Every service running on a server, whether it is essential or not, can potentially be targeted by attackers. When a service is enabled, it often opens one or more ports to communicate with other devices or systems. Each open port can be seen as an entry point, and attackers are known to scan networks for open ports that may correspond to vulnerable services. Services like FTP, Telnet, and others are common targets because they can be easily exploited if not configured correctly. Even if these services are not needed, they often remain enabled by default, leaving a server exposed to unnecessary risks. The first step in minimizing the attack surface is to conduct a thorough inventory of the services running on the server. Once this inventory is complete, administrators can evaluate which services are essential for the server's role and which can be safely disabled or removed.

Disabling unnecessary services is not just about reducing the number of potential attack vectors; it is also about simplifying the system. By stripping down a server to only the necessary services, administrators create a smaller, more manageable attack surface. A smaller attack surface means that fewer services are running, each with fewer potential vulnerabilities. This makes it much harder for attackers to find an exploitable weakness. When unnecessary services are disabled, there are fewer points for attackers to target, thus significantly improving the overall security posture of the system.

One of the most common services that is often left enabled on servers but is rarely needed is FTP (File Transfer Protocol). FTP was traditionally used to transfer files between systems, but today, there are more secure and efficient methods available, such as SFTP (Secure File Transfer Protocol) and SCP (Secure Copy Protocol). If FTP is not being used, it should be disabled immediately to avoid the risk of it being exploited. Similarly, Telnet is another legacy service that is often enabled by default on some servers, but it transmits data, including login credentials, in plaintext. This makes Telnet vulnerable to eavesdropping and man-in-the-middle attacks. Given that more secure alternatives, like SSH (Secure Shell), are widely available, there is no reason to keep Telnet active unless absolutely necessary. By disabling these legacy services, the server's security is immediately improved.

Another significant aspect of reducing the attack surface is controlling access to services. Many services, especially those designed for administrative purposes, can be misconfigured to allow broad access from the internet. Remote desktop services, for example, are frequently targeted by attackers, especially when weak passwords or default credentials are used. These services should be restricted to specific IP addresses, or better yet, completely disabled unless remote access is essential. Restricting access ensures that only authorized users can connect to the server, reducing the likelihood of a successful attack. For instance, if a server does not need to be remotely managed, remote desktop services should be completely turned off to prevent potential attackers from gaining unauthorized access.

Alongside disabling unnecessary services, another crucial part of minimizing the attack surface is ensuring that the services that remain enabled are securely configured. Even essential services, such as web servers or database servers, can become vulnerable if they are not properly configured. For example, many web servers come with default configurations that include unnecessary modules or features. These configurations can be exploited if attackers discover a flaw in them. It is essential to disable any unnecessary modules and limit the functionality of the server to only what is required. Additionally, the server should be configured with strong security settings, such as secure communication protocols, proper access controls, and up-to-date software patches.

The next step in reducing the attack surface is controlling open ports. Each service that runs on a server typically uses a specific port to communicate with the outside world. For instance, web servers typically use port 80 or 443, while email servers might use ports 25 or 587. If a port is open but the service using it is not required, it becomes an unnecessary point of entry for attackers. Network administrators should carefully review which ports are open and close those that are not needed. In many cases, services may have unused ports open by default, making them vulnerable to attacks. By ensuring that only the necessary ports are open, administrators can minimize the opportunity for an attack to occur.

In addition to reviewing open ports, administrators should also consider network segmentation as part of the overall strategy for reducing the attack surface. Segmenting the network into smaller, isolated subnets ensures that if an attacker does manage to exploit one server, they will not have easy access to the entire network. For example, placing web servers in a separate network zone from database servers prevents attackers who may compromise the web server from gaining immediate access to sensitive data stored on the database server. Network segmentation adds an additional layer of defense and limits the potential impact of a security breach.

It is also essential to perform regular audits of the services running on the server. As new patches and software updates are released, it is easy for administrators to overlook certain services that may have been enabled during the initial configuration. Conducting regular audits helps identify any services that have been inadvertently left running and provides an opportunity to disable them. This practice is especially important as the server evolves over time. As new applications are installed or existing ones are updated, they may introduce new services that need to be reviewed for necessity. Regular audits ensure that the server remains lean and that only essential services are running.

Minimizing the attack surface is an ongoing process that requires constant vigilance. Security threats evolve, and new vulnerabilities are discovered regularly. Therefore, administrators must stay updated on the latest security developments and continually assess the services running on their servers. By disabling unnecessary services, closing unnecessary ports, and securing the services that remain, administrators can significantly reduce the risk of a successful attack. The fewer entry points there are for attackers to exploit, the harder it becomes for them to penetrate the system. Ultimately, reducing the attack surface through careful management of services plays a critical role in the overall security of a server and the organization it supports.

Understanding the Role of Firewalls in System Hardening

Firewalls play a critical role in securing networked systems, acting as a protective barrier between trusted internal networks and untrusted external networks, such as the internet. Their purpose is to monitor and control incoming and outgoing network traffic based on predetermined security rules. By filtering traffic, firewalls can block malicious activity, unauthorized access, and potentially harmful communications, thereby significantly enhancing the overall security posture of a server. In the context of system hardening, firewalls are an essential component that helps reduce vulnerabilities and prevent attacks. Firewalls are versatile tools that can protect servers from various types of threats, including network-based attacks, data breaches, and other malicious activities.

A fundamental aspect of understanding firewalls is recognizing their role in controlling access to and from a network. In a typical network setup, a firewall serves as the first line of defense against external threats, ensuring that only authorized traffic can reach the server. By filtering data packets based on specified rules, firewalls determine whether to allow or block network traffic based on the IP address, port number, protocol, and other criteria. This process is essential in preventing unauthorized users from accessing sensitive systems and data. Additionally, firewalls provide protection against various types of attacks, such as Distributed Denial of Service (DDoS) attacks, where attackers flood a server with excessive traffic to overload the system and render it unavailable. By monitoring traffic patterns and applying predefined filtering rules, firewalls can help mitigate such attacks.

Firewalls also play an essential role in controlling access to server services, which is a critical aspect of system hardening. Many servers run multiple services, such as web servers, email servers, or database servers, each of which has its own set of communication ports. While these services are necessary for the server to function, they can also create vulnerabilities if not properly secured. Firewalls can be configured to allow only trusted IP addresses or specific ports, restricting access to the server's services. For example, a web server typically listens on port 80 for HTTP traffic or port 443 for HTTPS traffic. By configuring the firewall to only allow traffic on these specific ports, administrators can prevent unauthorized access to other services that may be running on the server. This level of granularity ensures that only legitimate traffic can access critical resources, reducing the attack surface and improving overall security.

In addition to filtering traffic based on IP addresses and ports, firewalls also examine the content of the traffic itself. Stateful firewalls, for instance, track the state of active connections and can detect abnormal patterns in communication, such as unsolicited incoming requests that are not part of an established session. This ability to examine traffic at a deeper level allows firewalls to block potential threats that may otherwise bypass traditional port-based filtering. For example, if an attacker attempts to initiate a connection from an unauthorized IP address or use an unusual protocol, the firewall can detect this and block the connection before it reaches the server. This added layer of security helps protect the system from more sophisticated attacks that may try to exploit vulnerabilities in the server or network services.

Another important aspect of firewalls in system hardening is their ability to prevent data exfiltration. Many cyberattacks are designed not only to gain unauthorized access to systems but also to steal sensitive information. Once an attacker has compromised a server, they may attempt to exfiltrate valuable data, such as customer information, financial records, or intellectual property. Firewalls can be configured to monitor outgoing traffic and prevent the unauthorized transmission of data. For instance, if an attacker gains access to a server and attempts to send sensitive data to an external location, the firewall can detect this unauthorized communication and block it. By controlling both inbound and outbound traffic, firewalls play a crucial role in preventing data breaches and protecting an organization's most valuable assets.

Moreover, firewalls can be an essential tool for segmenting a network. Network segmentation involves dividing a larger network into smaller, isolated segments to limit the spread of potential threats. Firewalls can be used to enforce these segments by controlling the traffic that is allowed between different parts of the network. For example, a server that hosts sensitive financial data may be placed in a separate network zone, and firewalls can be configured to only allow communication between this zone and trusted internal networks. By isolating critical systems and restricting access to only those who need it, organizations can greatly reduce the impact of a potential security breach. Even if an attacker compromises one part of the network, the segmented design helps contain the threat and prevents it from spreading throughout the entire system.

The importance of firewalls extends beyond just preventing attacks; they also provide valuable insight into the health and security of a network. Firewalls often include robust logging and monitoring capabilities that record details about traffic and network activity. These logs can be invaluable for detecting suspicious activity, identifying potential security incidents, and understanding the tactics used by attackers. For example, if an attacker attempts to brute-force login credentials or repeatedly probes specific ports for vulnerabilities, these activities are likely to be logged by the firewall. Administrators can review these logs to identify unusual patterns and take appropriate action to mitigate the threat. Additionally, firewall logs can help organizations comply with regulatory requirements, as they provide a detailed record of network activity and access attempts.

In terms of system hardening, it is crucial to configure firewalls to align with the principle of least privilege. This principle dictates that users and services should only be granted the minimum access necessary to perform their tasks. Similarly, firewalls should be configured to allow only the specific types of traffic required for the server's intended functions. For instance, if a server is only intended to serve web traffic, the firewall should be configured to block all other types of traffic, such as email or file transfer protocols. This minimizes the risk of unauthorized access and ensures that the server is not exposed to unnecessary threats. By applying the principle of least privilege to both user permissions and firewall configurations, administrators can create a more secure server environment.

It is also important to keep firewalls updated and properly maintained as part of system hardening. Cyber threats evolve constantly, and attackers continuously develop new techniques to bypass security measures. As a result, firewalls must be regularly updated to account for new vulnerabilities and attack vectors. This includes applying updates to the firewall software itself, as well as updating the rules and configurations that govern traffic filtering. By staying up-to-date with the latest security patches and best practices, administrators ensure that the firewall remains effective in defending against new and emerging threats.

The role of firewalls in system hardening cannot be underestimated. Firewalls are integral to protecting servers from unauthorized access, mitigating attacks, preventing data exfiltration, and providing valuable insight into network activity. By carefully configuring and maintaining firewalls, organizations can significantly enhance their overall security posture and reduce the risk of a successful attack. Firewalls are not a one-size-fits-all solution, and their configuration should be tailored to the specific needs and requirements of each server. When properly implemented, firewalls form an essential layer of defense, helping to protect servers from the many threats they face in today's digital landscape.

Implementing User Access Controls and Permissions

User access controls and permissions are fundamental components of a robust security framework, particularly when it comes to system hardening. In any organization, servers are critical assets that store sensitive data and provide vital services, making them prime targets for malicious actors. However, the security of a server does not rely solely on external defense mechanisms like firewalls and intrusion detection systems; internal measures, such as controlling user access and assigning appropriate permissions, are equally essential. Implementing effective user access controls and permissions ensures that only authorized individuals can access the server and its resources, while also limiting the scope of what they can do once inside. This minimizes the risk of unauthorized access, data breaches, and accidental or intentional misuse of the system.

One of the primary objectives of user access controls is to enforce the principle of least privilege. This principle dictates that users should only be granted the minimum level of access necessary to perform their job functions. By limiting users to the resources they absolutely need, organizations reduce the risk of both external and internal threats. For example, a user who only needs access to a specific set of files should not be granted full administrative privileges or access to other sensitive areas of the server. This reduces the potential damage if a user account is compromised or if the user makes an error. Furthermore, the principle of least privilege helps prevent the abuse of permissions, ensuring that no one has more access than they require to perform their work.

The process of implementing user access controls begins with defining user roles and responsibilities within the organization. These roles determine what level of access each user should be granted. For instance, a system administrator will require far more access to a server than a regular user who only needs access to a specific application or file. By categorizing users based on their roles, administrators can streamline the process of assigning permissions and ensure that access is granted according to the principle of least privilege. For each user role, administrators must carefully consider the specific tasks that the user will need to perform and grant permissions accordingly. This role-based approach to access control helps to ensure that users do not inadvertently receive excessive permissions.

Once user roles have been defined, the next step is to assign permissions to the server's resources. Permissions control what actions a user can perform on a resource, such as reading, writing, or executing files. For instance, a user who only needs to view files should be granted read-only permissions, while a user who needs to modify or create files will require write permissions. Similarly, administrators should also carefully manage execute permissions, which allow users to run programs or scripts. By precisely defining what each user can do with the resources they have access to, administrators can significantly reduce the risk of unauthorized or harmful actions.

In addition to defining roles and assigning permissions, it is crucial to implement strong authentication mechanisms for verifying the identity of users before granting them access. Passwords are the most common method of authentication, but they can be vulnerable to attacks if not properly managed. For example, weak or reused passwords can be easily guessed or cracked by attackers using brute-force methods. To enhance security, organizations should enforce strict password policies that require users to create complex, unique passwords and change them periodically. Furthermore, multi-factor authentication (MFA) should be implemented wherever possible. MFA adds an extra layer of security by requiring users to provide two or more forms of identification before accessing the system, such as a password and a one-time code sent to their mobile device.

Another important aspect of user access control is account management. This includes the process of creating, modifying, and disabling user accounts. When a new employee joins the organization, an account should be created for them with the appropriate permissions based on their role. As employees transition to different roles or leave the company, their access should be adjusted or revoked entirely. Failing to deactivate accounts for former employees or users who no longer need access can create security vulnerabilities, as these accounts may be exploited by malicious actors. Additionally, administrators should regularly audit user accounts to ensure that only active users have access and that their permissions are still appropriate for their current roles. Regular account reviews help to identify potential security risks and ensure that access controls remain aligned with the needs of the organization.

One of the challenges in managing user access is ensuring that permissions are granted and maintained in a way that minimizes human error. It is easy for administrators to inadvertently grant excessive permissions or forget to remove access when a user's role changes. To mitigate this risk, organizations should implement an automated process for permission management, such as using a centralized identity and access management (IAM) system. IAM systems allow administrators to manage user identities and permissions from a single interface, streamlining the process and reducing the likelihood of mistakes. These systems also help enforce security policies, such as password complexity requirements and MFA, across the organization.

Auditing and monitoring user activity are also critical aspects of implementing effective access controls. Even with the best security policies in place, malicious or negligent behavior can still occur. Therefore, it is important to continuously monitor user activity on the server and investigate any unusual or suspicious actions. For example, if a user suddenly attempts to access files or systems they do not normally interact with, this may indicate a compromised account or unauthorized access attempt. Regular logging of user activity and reviewing these logs allows administrators to detect security incidents early and take corrective action. Additionally, auditing user activity helps organizations meet compliance requirements, as many regulations mandate the monitoring and logging of user access to sensitive data.

In addition to monitoring user activity, administrators should implement clear policies for handling and responding to security incidents involving user access. In the event of a breach or suspicious behavior, organizations must have a well-defined process for investigating the issue, revoking access if necessary, and mitigating any damage. For example, if an employee's account is compromised, administrators should immediately disable the account, reset the password, and investigate whether any sensitive data has been accessed or exfiltrated. By having a clear response plan in place, organizations can minimize the impact of security incidents and recover more quickly.

Finally, as organizations continue to adopt new technologies, it is essential to consider how emerging trends affect user access controls. Cloud computing, for instance, introduces new challenges in managing user permissions across multiple platforms and services. The increasing use of mobile devices and remote work also requires additional considerations for securing user access from various locations and devices. In these cases, organizations should implement access controls that are flexible enough to accommodate these changes while maintaining a high level of security.

The implementation of user access controls and permissions is a critical component of system hardening. By carefully defining user roles, assigning the appropriate permissions, and enforcing strong authentication measures, organizations can significantly reduce the risk of unauthorized access and data breaches. Proper account management, auditing, and monitoring of user activity further enhance the security of the system, ensuring that only authorized individuals can access sensitive resources. Through diligent attention to user access controls and permissions, organizations can create a more secure and resilient server environment.

Securing Server Configurations and Settings

Securing server configurations and settings is one of the most critical aspects of system hardening. Servers are often the backbone of an organization's digital infrastructure, providing essential services, hosting critical data, and managing communication between internal and external systems. However, they are also prime targets for cyberattacks due to their central role in business operations. When misconfigured, servers can leave significant vulnerabilities that attackers can exploit, leading to data breaches, system downtime, or unauthorized access. As such, securing the configurations and settings of a server is not merely an additional step in hardening; it is a fundamental requirement for ensuring that the server is resilient to a wide range of cyber threats.

The first step in securing server configurations is to ensure that the server is running only the necessary services and that these services are properly configured. By default, many server operating systems come with a wide array of services enabled, some of which may not be necessary for the server's intended role. Services like FTP, Telnet, and remote desktop may be enabled by default but are often not required for the server's operation. Leaving these services enabled unnecessarily opens additional attack vectors for malicious actors. For example, Telnet transmits data, including login credentials, in plaintext, making it vulnerable to eavesdropping attacks. Similarly, if services like FTP are not configured securely, they can be exploited for unauthorized access. Therefore, administrators should carefully assess the server's required services and disable or remove any unnecessary ones. This practice not only reduces the attack surface but also improves the overall efficiency of the server by limiting the number of active processes.

Securing server configurations also involves ensuring that the server is set up to restrict unauthorized access and limit permissions. By configuring proper access control measures, administrators can prevent unauthorized users from gaining entry to sensitive parts of the server. One of the most effective ways to do this is by configuring strong password policies. Passwords are often the first line of defense against unauthorized access, and weak or easily guessable passwords can make it significantly easier for attackers to compromise a system. Administrators should enforce password complexity requirements, ensuring that passwords are sufficiently long and contain a mix of letters, numbers, and special characters. Password expiration policies should also be implemented to ensure that passwords are periodically changed and not reused over time. In addition, multi-factor authentication (MFA) should be enabled wherever possible, adding an extra layer of security by requiring users to provide more than just a password to access the system.

Another critical element of securing server configurations is ensuring that the server is protected by a properly configured firewall. Firewalls serve as a first line of defense by controlling incoming and outgoing traffic based on predefined rules. By configuring the firewall to block all traffic except for specific, authorized connections, administrators can greatly reduce the chances of an attacker gaining access to the server. The firewall should only allow the services required for the server to function and should block all other ports and protocols that are unnecessary. Additionally, administrators should configure the firewall to log and monitor all traffic to identify any suspicious activity or unauthorized access attempts. The combination of restricting unnecessary services and properly configuring the firewall creates a robust barrier against external threats.

One important security measure often overlooked is securing the server's file and directory permissions. Servers store a vast amount of data, and much of it is sensitive or confidential in nature. If these files are not properly protected, they can be accessed or modified by unauthorized individuals, either intentionally or unintentionally. To mitigate this risk, administrators must ensure that file and directory permissions are configured according to the principle of least privilege. This principle dictates that users should only be granted the minimum level of access necessary for them to perform their job functions. By setting restrictive permissions on sensitive files and directories, administrators can ensure that only authorized users have access to critical data. Additionally, file integrity monitoring tools can be employed to detect any unauthorized changes to key files or configurations, alerting administrators to potential security breaches.

Regularly updating server software and applying security patches is also an essential component of securing server configurations. Software vendors regularly release patches and updates to address known vulnerabilities, and failing to apply these updates in a timely manner can leave the server exposed to exploitation. Many cyberattacks are the result of unpatched vulnerabilities in the server's operating system, applications, or third-party software. To reduce the risk of these types of attacks, administrators should establish a process for regularly reviewing and applying patches. In some cases, automated patch management systems can be implemented to streamline this process, ensuring that the server remains up to date with the latest security fixes. However, it is equally important to test patches in a controlled environment before deploying them to production systems, as some updates may introduce compatibility issues or cause other problems.

Secure server settings also require proper logging and monitoring configurations. Keeping detailed logs of server activity is crucial for identifying potential security incidents and investigating the root cause of any breaches that occur. Logging can provide insight into which users are accessing the server, what actions they are performing, and whether any unauthorized attempts to access the system have been made. This information can be invaluable for detecting and responding to security incidents in real time. It is also essential to configure the server to store logs securely, ensuring that log files cannot be tampered with or deleted by attackers. Logs should be stored in a centralized location where they can be easily accessed for review and analysis. Regular monitoring of these logs allows administrators to detect abnormal activity patterns, such as failed login attempts or unusual traffic spikes, which may indicate that the server is under attack.

Securing server configurations also includes implementing proper network security measures. In addition to firewalls, administrators should configure intrusion detection and prevention systems (IDPS) to detect and respond to suspicious network activity. These systems can analyze network traffic for signs of known attack patterns and block malicious traffic before it reaches the server. Additionally, network segmentation can be used to isolate critical systems and restrict access to sensitive resources. For example, servers that store sensitive data can be placed in a separate network zone, accessible only by trusted users or devices, while less sensitive systems can be placed in a different zone. This helps to limit the potential impact of a security breach and ensures that critical data remains protected.

In addition to securing the server's internal settings, administrators must also ensure that the server is physically protected. Physical security is often overlooked in discussions of system hardening, but it is an essential aspect of securing a server. Servers should be housed in secure, access-controlled locations, such as data centers, where only authorized personnel can physically interact with the equipment. Any attempt to tamper with the server's hardware or access it directly can compromise the integrity of the system and the data it contains.

Securing server configurations and settings is an ongoing process that requires continuous attention and vigilance. As new threats emerge and the server environment evolves, administrators must regularly reassess and update configurations to ensure they remain secure. By implementing a strong foundation of secure configurations, organizations can significantly reduce the risk of security breaches and ensure that their servers remain resilient to cyber threats.

Strengthening Password Policies for Server Accounts

One of the most crucial aspects of securing a server is implementing strong password policies for server accounts. Servers are the backbone of an organization's IT infrastructure, holding critical data, managing applications, and facilitating communication between systems. With such a central role, servers are prime targets for cyberattacks, and weak passwords are one of the most common entry points for attackers. A password is often the first line of defense in protecting access to server accounts, making it essential to enforce stringent password policies. Strong password policies reduce the risk of unauthorized access, ensure the integrity of server accounts, and contribute to the overall security of the system.

The foundation of a strong password policy begins with password complexity. Passwords that are too simple or easy to guess, such as "123456" or "password," are highly vulnerable to brute-force attacks and other methods of compromise. A weak password can be cracked in seconds using automated tools that systematically attempt every possible combination until the correct one is found. To strengthen password security, administrators should enforce rules that require passwords to meet certain complexity criteria. For instance, passwords should include a mix of uppercase and lowercase letters, numbers, and special characters. This makes the password harder to guess or crack using automated tools, significantly improving the security of the server account.

In addition to complexity, password length is another critical factor in strengthening password policies. Research has shown that longer passwords are much more secure than shorter ones. A password that is at least 12 to 16 characters long provides a much larger possible keyspace for attackers to try and increases the time it would take for a brute-force attack to succeed. Longer passwords are exponentially more difficult to crack compared to shorter ones, as each additional character significantly increases the number of possible combinations. Therefore, administrators should set minimum password length requirements to ensure that users create sufficiently strong passwords that are difficult to crack.

Equally important to password complexity and length is the enforcement of password expiration policies. A password that remains unchanged for long periods is more likely to be compromised, either through brute-force attacks or by an attacker gaining access to it via other means. Regularly changing passwords ensures that even if an attacker manages to obtain a password, they will not be able to use it for an extended period. Administrators should set a maximum password age, requiring users to change their passwords periodically. This reduces the risk of a password being exposed and used maliciously over time. Typically, a password expiration period of 60 to 90 days is considered best practice. However, administrators should balance this with user convenience, ensuring that the expiration period is frequent enough to improve security without causing unnecessary disruption.

Alongside expiration policies, password history policies are also an essential component of a strong password policy. Without a password history policy, users may recycle old passwords or use variations of the same password, which can make it easier for attackers to guess or crack their credentials. A password history policy prevents users from reusing their previous passwords for a specified number of password changes, further reducing the likelihood of an attacker exploiting a reused or similar password. This policy ensures that users adopt truly new passwords every time they are required to change them, further strengthening the overall security of the server account.

An often-overlooked aspect of strengthening password security is educating users about the importance of choosing strong passwords and following password policies. Even the most stringent password policies will fail if users are not aware of the risks associated with weak passwords or the importance of following the rules. Security awareness training should be provided to all users, particularly those with access to server accounts. This training should emphasize the significance of creating strong, unique passwords, the dangers of reusing passwords across multiple accounts, and how to securely manage and store passwords. Additionally, users should be educated about the risks of phishing and social engineering attacks, which can trick them into disclosing their credentials. Empowering users with the knowledge to follow password policies correctly can make a significant difference in securing server accounts.

Another crucial aspect of strengthening password policies is the use of multi-factor authentication (MFA). While strong passwords are essential, they alone may not be sufficient to protect sensitive server accounts. Multi-factor authentication provides an added layer of security by requiring users to present additional evidence of their identity beyond just a password. This could include something they have, such as a mobile device or a hardware token, or something they are, such as a fingerprint or other biometric data. Even if an attacker manages to compromise a password, MFA makes it significantly more difficult for them to gain unauthorized access to the server account. Implementing MFA for all server accounts, particularly for administrators and users with access to sensitive data, is one of the most effective ways to enhance password security.

In addition to MFA, password managers can be used to help users manage their passwords securely. Given the increasing complexity and length of passwords required by modern password policies, it can be difficult for users to remember all of their credentials. This can lead to the temptation to write passwords down or reuse them across multiple accounts, both of which are significant security risks. Password managers securely store and generate complex, unique passwords for each account, making it easier for users to follow password policies without compromising security. By using a password manager, users can ensure that they follow best practices while keeping their credentials secure and manageable.

Enforcing account lockout policies is another important measure for strengthening password security. Brute-force attacks, in which attackers attempt to guess passwords by trying numerous combinations in quick succession, are one of the most common methods used to compromise server accounts. Account lockout policies can help prevent these attacks by temporarily disabling accounts after a certain number of failed login attempts. This reduces the effectiveness of brute-force attacks and provides an additional layer of protection for server accounts. Administrators should configure account lockout thresholds to strike a balance between security and usability, ensuring that legitimate users are not inconvenienced while protecting against malicious login attempts.

Server administrators should also regularly audit user accounts and their associated password policies to ensure compliance. Over time, users may fail to update their passwords or adhere to password policies, potentially creating vulnerabilities. By conducting regular audits, administrators can identify accounts that do not comply with the password policies and take corrective actions as necessary. These audits help to ensure that the password policies remain effective and that any potential security gaps are addressed before they can be exploited by attackers.

The enforcement of strong password policies is a cornerstone of securing server accounts. By ensuring that passwords are complex, long, unique, and regularly updated, administrators can greatly reduce the risk of unauthorized access. Implementing additional measures such as multi-factor authentication, password managers, and account lockout policies further enhances password security and provides layers of protection against cyber threats. Ultimately, strengthening password policies helps to ensure that server accounts remain secure, reducing the likelihood of a breach and safeguarding sensitive data and systems.

Limiting Remote Access to Servers

Remote access to servers is an essential capability for many organizations, allowing administrators to manage, troubleshoot, and perform updates on systems from virtually anywhere in the world. However, while remote access is beneficial for operational flexibility, it also opens the door to significant security risks. If not properly controlled, remote access can provide malicious actors with opportunities to infiltrate servers and compromise sensitive data. Therefore, limiting remote access to servers is one of the most important steps in securing server environments. Implementing strong access controls, monitoring, and secure communication protocols can significantly reduce the likelihood of unauthorized access and ensure that only authorized users are able to connect remotely.

The first step in limiting remote access is to assess whether remote access is even necessary for a particular server. Some servers may not require remote access at all, and if this is the case, it is crucial to disable all remote access capabilities. Servers that are entirely self-contained and do not need to be accessed from outside their local network should be configured to block any external connection attempts. Disabling unnecessary remote access services eliminates a significant attack vector, as it ensures that external threats cannot exploit remote access protocols to gain entry. For example, if a server only needs to be accessed locally, then services like SSH, RDP, or VPN should be disabled to prevent any remote login attempts.

For servers where remote access is necessary, administrators should implement strong authentication mechanisms to ensure that only authorized users can access the system. Password-based authentication alone is insufficient, as passwords can be cracked or stolen by attackers. Multi-factor authentication (MFA) provides an additional layer of security by requiring users to provide two or more forms of identification before being granted access. This could include something the user knows, such as a password, and something they have, such as a mobile device or hardware token that generates a time-sensitive code. By requiring multiple forms of identification, MFA significantly reduces the risk of unauthorized access, as even if an attacker compromises a password, they would still need the second factor to successfully log in.

In addition to multi-factor authentication, administrators should enforce the use of strong, unique passwords for all users with remote access to the server. Passwords should be sufficiently complex to prevent attackers from easily guessing or brute-forcing them. A strong password typically contains a mix of uppercase and lowercase letters, numbers, and special characters, and should be at least 12 to 16 characters in length. To ensure that users do not reuse passwords across multiple services, administrators should implement password expiration policies and require users to change their passwords regularly. Additionally, it is essential to educate users about the importance of choosing strong passwords and adhering to the organization's password policy.

Another critical aspect of limiting remote access is restricting which users are allowed to connect remotely. Not all users need remote access, and unnecessary accounts should be disabled or removed. The principle of least privilege should always be followed when granting remote access, ensuring that users only have access to the resources they need to perform their job functions. This principle limits the potential damage that could be caused by a compromised account. For example, an employee who only needs to access a specific application should not be granted administrative access to the entire server. By minimizing the number of users who have remote access, administrators reduce the likelihood of unauthorized access and limit the attack surface of the server.

In addition to limiting user access, administrators should carefully control the methods through which remote access is granted. One of the most common methods for remote access is Secure Shell (SSH) for Linux-based servers and Remote Desktop Protocol (RDP) for Windows-based servers. While both of these protocols are essential tools for managing servers remotely, they can also be exploited by attackers if not properly secured. SSH and RDP should only be accessible through secure, encrypted communication channels to prevent data from being intercepted during transmission. Configuring SSH to use key-based authentication instead of password-based authentication adds an additional layer of security, as SSH keys are far more difficult to compromise than passwords. Similarly, RDP should be configured to use Network Level Authentication (NLA), which requires users to authenticate before a full connection is established.

Firewall rules play a vital role in limiting remote access. By configuring firewalls to only allow connections from trusted IP addresses, administrators can significantly reduce the number of potential remote access points. For example, if remote access is only needed from specific locations or IP addresses, the firewall should be configured to block all other incoming connections. This prevents attackers from attempting to connect from untrusted locations or using tools like IP spoofing to bypass firewall restrictions. If dynamic IP addresses are involved, VPNs can be used to ensure that remote connections are encrypted and restricted to authorized networks.

To further strengthen security, administrators should implement a Virtual Private Network (VPN) for remote access. A VPN creates a secure tunnel between the user's device and the server, encrypting all data transmitted between the two endpoints. By requiring users to connect to the server through a VPN, organizations can ensure that remote access is encrypted and protected from interception. VPNs also provide an additional layer of security by requiring users to authenticate before establishing a connection, ensuring that only authorized individuals can access the network. Moreover, VPNs allow administrators to monitor remote access and restrict access to specific resources based on the user's role or location.

Another crucial measure to limit remote access is logging and monitoring all remote connection attempts. Server logs can provide invaluable information about who is attempting to access the server, from where, and when. By reviewing these logs regularly, administrators can detect suspicious activity, such as failed login attempts, logins from unfamiliar IP addresses, or login attempts during unusual hours. These logs can help administrators quickly identify potential security incidents and take action to prevent unauthorized access. Additionally, administrators should set up alerts for suspicious activities so that they are notified immediately if any unusual behavior is detected. Early detection of unauthorized access attempts allows for a rapid response, such as locking down the server, disabling compromised accounts, or implementing more stringent access controls.

Time-based access restrictions can also be an effective way to limit remote access. For example, if remote access is only necessary during business hours, administrators can configure the server to reject remote connection attempts outside of those hours. This reduces the time window in which attackers can attempt to exploit remote access. Time-based restrictions can be applied to both user accounts and remote access services, ensuring that the server remains secure even when access is not required. Additionally, temporary access can be granted for specific tasks or projects, and access can be revoked once the task is completed.

Finally, remote access should be continuously reviewed and updated to account for changes in the network, user roles, and the threat landscape. As an organization grows and evolves, new remote access needs may arise, and old configurations may become outdated or insecure. Administrators should regularly audit remote access configurations, update access controls, and ensure that remote access policies align with the organization's current security requirements. Regular reviews ensure that only authorized individuals can access the server and that remote access is managed according to the latest security standards.

By carefully controlling and limiting remote access to servers, organizations can significantly reduce the risk of unauthorized access and protect sensitive data and systems from cyber threats. Implementing strong authentication, using secure communication protocols, configuring firewalls, and monitoring remote access are all essential components of a comprehensive security strategy. Limiting remote access is not only about reducing the number of potential entry points but also about ensuring that only trusted users and systems can connect to the server. In doing so, organizations can enhance the overall security of their IT infrastructure and minimize the risk of successful cyberattacks.

Using Secure Communication Protocols for Server Connections

In today's interconnected world, communication between servers, users, and other systems is essential for the functioning of most organizations. Servers store critical data, process information, and provide services to other systems, making them attractive targets for cybercriminals. If communication between these systems is not properly secured, it can expose sensitive data to interception, tampering, and unauthorized access. Therefore, using secure communication protocols is a fundamental step in protecting the integrity and confidentiality of server connections. Secure protocols ensure that data is transmitted safely, preventing attackers from gaining access to sensitive information while in transit.

One of the most widely used secure communication protocols is Transport Layer Security (TLS), which ensures that data transmitted over a network is encrypted and protected from eavesdropping and tampering. TLS operates between the transport layer and the application layer in the OSI model, providing encryption for protocols like HTTP (HTTP over TLS is commonly referred to as HTTPS). When a server and a client communicate using TLS, the data is encrypted, ensuring that even if an attacker intercepts the communication, they will not be able to read or manipulate the data. This encryption prevents man-in-the-middle attacks, where an attacker might intercept and modify data in transit between two parties. TLS also ensures the integrity of the data, meaning that it cannot be altered during transmission without detection. Implementing TLS for all server connections, especially for web servers and applications that handle sensitive data, is a crucial step in securing communication.

Another important secure communication protocol is Secure Shell (SSH), which provides a secure method for accessing remote servers over a network. SSH replaces older, insecure protocols like Telnet and rlogin, which transmit data in plaintext and expose it to potential interception. SSH uses strong encryption to protect data, ensuring that login credentials and commands are not exposed during remote sessions. In addition to encrypting the communication, SSH also provides authentication mechanisms that help verify the identity of the user connecting to the server. This can include password-based authentication, public key authentication, or a combination of both. SSH is widely used by system administrators and other users who need secure access to remote servers, and it is essential for protecting server configurations and preventing unauthorized access.

When securing server connections, it is also important to use secure versions of file transfer protocols. File Transfer Protocol (FTP) is commonly used to transfer files between systems, but it transmits data in plaintext, making it vulnerable to eavesdropping and attacks. To mitigate this risk, administrators should use Secure FTP (SFTP) or FTP Secure (FTPS). SFTP uses the SSH protocol to encrypt data during transmission, ensuring that files are transferred securely between servers or between a client and a server. FTPS, on the other hand, uses TLS or SSL to secure the communication between the FTP client and server. Both of these protocols provide encryption, ensuring that data is not exposed to unauthorized parties during the file transfer process. When sensitive data is being transferred between servers or clients, using SFTP or FTPS instead of traditional FTP is a critical step in securing communication and protecting data.

In addition to securing communication between servers and clients, securing communication between servers within an organization's network is also important. Many organizations rely on internal communication between servers to support business operations, such as database queries, file sharing, and application interactions. If these internal communications are not encrypted, they can be intercepted by attackers who gain access to the internal network. For this reason, it is important to use secure communication protocols within the internal network as well. One approach is to implement IPsec (Internet Protocol Security), which provides encryption and authentication for IP packets transmitted between devices on a network. IPsec can be used to secure communication between servers, routers, and other network devices, ensuring that sensitive data remains protected even within the internal network. By encrypting internal communications, organizations can minimize the risk of data breaches caused by internal threats or unauthorized access to the network.

When configuring secure communication protocols, it is essential to ensure that the latest versions of the protocols are used. Protocols like TLS, SSH, and SFTP have undergone multiple revisions over the years, with each version providing improved security features and addressing vulnerabilities found in previous versions. For example, earlier versions of SSL (Secure Sockets Layer), the predecessor to TLS, are now considered insecure and should no longer be used. Similarly, older versions of SSH may lack modern encryption standards, making them vulnerable to attacks. Administrators should always configure servers to use the latest stable versions of these protocols to ensure that they are protected from known vulnerabilities. Regularly updating server software and reviewing the configurations of secure communication protocols helps to keep the server environment secure and resilient to attacks.

While encryption is a critical component of securing communication, it is equally important to properly configure the servers and applications that use secure communication protocols. For example, SSL/TLS certificates must be properly installed and configured to ensure that encrypted connections are established correctly. Servers should be configured to use strong encryption algorithms, such as AES (Advanced Encryption Standard), and avoid weak or deprecated algorithms that may be vulnerable to attacks. Additionally, administrators should configure servers to require strong client authentication, ensuring that only authorized clients can establish secure connections. For SSH, this means disabling weak authentication methods like password-based authentication and instead using public key authentication. Properly configuring secure communication protocols not only ensures encryption but also strengthens the overall security of the server by preventing misconfigurations that could expose the system to risks.

Another important consideration when using secure communication protocols is performance. Encryption, while essential for protecting data, can introduce overhead that affects the performance of the server and the speed of communication. However, with modern hardware and optimized algorithms, the performance impact of encryption is minimal, and the security benefits far outweigh any potential slowdown. That said, administrators should still monitor server performance and adjust configurations as necessary to ensure that the server can handle the required load while maintaining secure communication. Load balancing, hardware acceleration for encryption tasks, and optimizing network configurations are some strategies that can help mitigate any performance issues caused by the use of secure communication protocols.

In addition to using secure communication protocols, administrators should also implement monitoring and logging to track communication activities on the server. Monitoring tools can help detect unauthorized attempts to establish connections, alert administrators to suspicious activity, and provide a detailed record of communication events. Logs should include information about the source and destination of communication, the type of protocol used, and any errors or anomalies encountered during the connection process. Regularly reviewing these logs can help identify potential security threats and ensure that secure communication protocols are being used properly.

By utilizing secure communication protocols like TLS, SSH, SFTP, and IPsec, organizations can significantly reduce the risk of unauthorized access, data breaches, and other cyberattacks. These protocols provide encryption, authentication, and data integrity, ensuring that sensitive information remains protected while in transit. Proper configuration, regular updates, and ongoing monitoring are essential to maintaining the security of server connections. Ultimately, secure communication protocols form the foundation of a strong security posture, helping organizations safeguard their data and systems from external and internal threats.

The Role of Encryption in Securing Server Data

In today's digital landscape, data is one of the most valuable assets an organization possesses. Servers are responsible for storing, processing, and transmitting vast amounts of sensitive information, including personal data, financial records, intellectual property, and business secrets. As a result, ensuring the confidentiality and integrity of this data is paramount to an organization's overall security strategy. Encryption plays a crucial role in securing server data by transforming it into a format that is unreadable without the appropriate decryption key. This process not only protects data from unauthorized access but also ensures that it remains intact and unaltered during transmission. The role of encryption in securing server data cannot be overstated, as it provides an essential layer of protection against cyberattacks, data breaches, and other malicious activities.

At its core, encryption is the process of converting plaintext data into ciphertext using an algorithm and an encryption key. The encrypted data can only be read or restored to its original form by someone who possesses the correct decryption key. This ensures that even if an attacker intercepts the data while it is in transit or gains access to the storage system, they will not be able to read or manipulate the information. Encryption serves as a critical tool in protecting sensitive data, especially in an age where cybercriminals are increasingly targeting organizations with sophisticated methods, including man-in-the-middle attacks, phishing, and ransomware.

One of the primary benefits of encryption is that it protects data during transmission. When data is sent over a network, whether it's a local area network (LAN), wide area network (WAN), or the internet, it is susceptible to interception. Without encryption, attackers could easily intercept and read unprotected data packets as they travel through the network. This is particularly concerning when dealing with sensitive data, such as login credentials, financial information, or personal identifiers. By encrypting data before it is transmitted, encryption ensures that even if data is intercepted, it remains unreadable. Protocols like Transport Layer Security (TLS) and Secure Socket Layer (SSL) are widely used for encrypting communication between clients and servers, especially for web traffic. These protocols provide an encrypted channel for data to travel through, making it almost impossible for attackers to decrypt the information without the correct keys.

Encryption also protects data at rest, which refers to data stored on a physical device or server. Servers store vast amounts of data, including backups, databases, and application files. If this data is not properly encrypted, it becomes vulnerable to unauthorized access, especially if the physical device is stolen, lost, or accessed by a malicious actor. Hard drives, flash drives, and cloud storage can all be targeted by attackers seeking to steal sensitive information. Full disk encryption (FDE) is one method of protecting data at rest, where all the data on the disk is encrypted. This ensures that even if an attacker gains access to the physical device, they cannot read the data without the decryption key. File-level encryption, on the other hand, encrypts specific files or directories that contain sensitive data, offering a more granular level of protection. Regardless of the method, encrypting data at rest ensures that data remains secure even if it is no longer actively being used or transmitted.

In addition to protecting data during transmission and at rest, encryption is also vital for securing user credentials and authentication processes. Server environments often rely on password-based authentication mechanisms to verify the identity of users. However, storing passwords in plaintext can expose them to unauthorized access. If an attacker gains access to a server's database, they may be able to retrieve these passwords and compromise user accounts. To prevent this, passwords should always be encrypted using strong hashing algorithms, such as bcrypt or Argon2, before being stored in the server's database. This way, even if an attacker successfully gains access to the database, they will not be able to retrieve the original passwords. Password encryption also helps prevent other types of attacks, such as brute-force attacks and rainbow table attacks, which attempt to reverse-engineer encrypted passwords by comparing them to precomputed values.

Encryption plays a crucial role in ensuring the integrity of data as well. In addition to making data unreadable to unauthorized parties, encryption also helps protect data from tampering or modification during transmission. When data is encrypted, it is typically accompanied by a cryptographic hash, which is a fixed-length string of characters generated by applying a hash function to the data. The hash serves as a digital fingerprint of the data, ensuring that it has not been altered during transmission. If the data is modified in any way, the hash will no longer match the original hash value, indicating that the integrity of the data has been compromised. This feature of encryption is particularly important when transmitting sensitive data, such as software updates or financial transactions, where even the slightest modification could result in significant consequences.

In addition to protecting the data itself, encryption also helps ensure compliance with data protection regulations. Many industries, such as finance, healthcare, and e-commerce, are subject to strict data protection laws and regulations, such as the General Data Protection Regulation (GDPR) and the Health Insurance Portability and Accountability Act (HIPAA). These regulations often require organizations to implement encryption to safeguard personal data and prevent data breaches. For example, GDPR mandates that personal data must be encrypted both in transit and at rest to ensure that it remains protected. By using encryption to protect server data, organizations can meet regulatory requirements and avoid potential fines or legal repercussions resulting from data breaches.

Another significant benefit of encryption is that it helps protect data in the event of a server breach. While encryption does not prevent breaches from occurring, it significantly mitigates the impact of a breach by making stolen data useless without the decryption key. In the case of a server breach, encrypted data remains protected, reducing the risk of sensitive information being exposed or stolen. This is particularly important for organizations that store large volumes of personal or financial data. Encryption ensures that even if an attacker gains access to a server, they cannot use the stolen data for malicious purposes, as it remains encrypted and unreadable.

Encryption is not without its challenges, however. One of the main concerns with encryption is the management of encryption keys. Encryption relies on keys to both encrypt and decrypt data, and if these keys are lost, compromised, or poorly managed, the data becomes inaccessible or vulnerable. Therefore, it is critical for organizations to implement a robust key management system (KMS) to securely store and manage encryption keys. Key management should include access controls to limit who can access the keys, regular audits to ensure proper usage, and backup procedures to prevent data loss in case of key failure.

In addition to key management, encryption can also introduce performance overhead, particularly in environments that handle large volumes of data or require real-time access to information. Encrypting and decrypting data requires processing power, which can slow down server performance. However, modern hardware and optimized algorithms have significantly reduced the performance impact of encryption, and the security benefits far outweigh the potential slowdowns. Administrators should balance encryption requirements with server performance needs, ensuring that encryption does not unduly impact the functionality of the server while still providing robust data protection.

Encryption plays a vital role in securing server data by ensuring the confidentiality, integrity, and authenticity of information. By encrypting data in transit and at rest, organizations can protect sensitive data from unauthorized access and ensure that it remains intact and unaltered during transmission. Encryption also helps organizations meet regulatory requirements and protect against the consequences of data breaches. While encryption can introduce challenges, such as key management and performance considerations, its benefits in securing server data are indispensable in today's threat landscape.

Regular Patching and Updates to Prevent Exploits

In the ever-evolving landscape of cybersecurity, regular patching and updates are essential practices for maintaining the security and integrity of servers. Servers play a pivotal role in storing, processing, and transmitting sensitive data, making them prime targets for cybercriminals. Vulnerabilities in server software, operating systems, and applications provide attackers with an opportunity to exploit weaknesses in the system, gaining unauthorized access or causing significant damage. Patch management is one of the most effective ways to prevent these exploits, as it addresses known vulnerabilities by providing fixes that close security gaps and improve overall system stability. Without regular patching, organizations expose themselves to significant risks, as attackers continuously search for unpatched systems to exploit.

At its core, patching involves applying updates provided by software vendors or developers to fix security vulnerabilities and bugs within a system. When a vulnerability is discovered, vendors typically release a security patch or update to address the issue. These patches are designed to correct flaws that could be exploited by malicious actors, thus preventing the possibility of a successful attack. However, many organizations fail to apply patches in a timely manner, leaving their systems exposed to known threats. Cybercriminals often scan networks for unpatched systems and exploit these vulnerabilities before organizations can address them. Regular patching is crucial to reducing the attack surface of a server, ensuring that known vulnerabilities cannot be exploited to compromise the system.

One of the primary reasons regular patching is necessary is that cybercriminals frequently target known vulnerabilities in widely used software. Popular operating systems, applications, and web servers are frequent targets because attackers are aware that many systems are running outdated versions of software that are vulnerable to known exploits. For instance, in the past, vulnerabilities in widely used software like Microsoft Windows, Apache web servers, and MySQL databases have been targeted by attackers who deploy malicious code, ransomware, or other types of malware. Once an attacker gains access to a vulnerable server, they can steal sensitive data, alter configurations, or even take control of the system. By ensuring that servers are regularly updated with the latest patches, administrators can reduce the risk of these types of attacks, making it much harder for attackers to exploit vulnerabilities in the system.

Another important aspect of patch management is addressing not just critical security vulnerabilities but also performance and functionality improvements. Many patches are not only designed to fix security issues but also to improve the overall stability, performance, and functionality of a system. Software vendors often release updates to enhance performance, fix bugs, and provide new features. While these updates may not always be related to security, they can help optimize the server's operations, making it more efficient and reliable. Applying these updates ensures that the server operates at its full potential, reducing the chances of downtime or operational issues that can arise from running outdated software.

Despite the clear benefits of patching, many organizations fail to implement an effective patch management strategy. One reason for this is the complexity and time-consuming nature of patching, especially in large environments where multiple servers are involved. In some cases, organizations may lack the resources or personnel to keep up with the constant stream of updates released by vendors. Additionally, applying patches to production systems can sometimes cause disruptions, such as system downtime or compatibility issues with other software. As a result, administrators may delay or neglect patching, leaving their systems vulnerable to attacks. However, the risks of not patching far outweigh the potential inconveniences, as unpatched systems can quickly become targets for cybercriminals.

To mitigate the challenges associated with patch management, organizations can implement automated patching solutions. These solutions can help streamline the process of identifying, testing, and deploying patches to servers, reducing the manual effort required by administrators. Automated patch management tools can scan systems for missing patches, download the necessary updates, and deploy them to the appropriate servers without requiring significant intervention. This ensures that patches are applied promptly, reducing the window of vulnerability between when a patch is released and when it is applied. Automated systems also allow for better tracking and reporting, helping administrators maintain a clear record of the patches that have been applied and those that are still outstanding.

It is also essential to test patches before deploying them to production servers. While patches are designed to address vulnerabilities, they can sometimes introduce compatibility issues or cause other unforeseen problems with existing software or configurations. By testing patches in a controlled environment before applying them to live systems, administrators can ensure that they will not disrupt operations or introduce new vulnerabilities. Testing patches is particularly important in environments that rely on complex, custom configurations or have a large number of applications and services running. In these cases, even a small change can have far-reaching effects. By thoroughly testing patches in a staging environment, administrators can identify and resolve any potential issues before applying them to production systems.

One of the challenges in maintaining a regular patching schedule is the need to balance security with operational continuity. While applying patches is crucial for securing servers, administrators must also consider the potential impact of updates on system performance and availability. Some patches, especially those related to operating systems, can require server restarts or downtime. For critical servers that provide essential services, such as databases or web applications, downtime can result in significant disruptions to business operations. To mitigate this risk, organizations should develop patching schedules that minimize the impact on system availability. Patching can be done during off-peak hours or during maintenance windows to ensure that the servers remain operational while still being updated regularly.

Furthermore, patching should be seen as an ongoing process rather than a one-time task. As new vulnerabilities are discovered, vendors continue to release new patches and updates. Cybercriminals are always looking for unpatched systems to exploit, which means that patch management should be integrated into the overall security strategy of the organization. Administrators must continuously monitor for new patches, test them, and deploy them promptly to ensure that servers remain secure. Regular patch audits should be conducted to ensure that all critical patches are applied and that no systems are left vulnerable. The goal is to make patching a routine part of system administration rather than an afterthought.

In addition to patching operating systems and applications, organizations should also patch third-party software, libraries, and frameworks that are used by servers. Many servers rely on third-party components, such as content management systems, web frameworks, and database engines, to provide additional functionality. These components can also contain vulnerabilities that need to be addressed through patching. Administrators should ensure that all software running on the server, including third-party tools and services, is kept up to date with the latest security patches. Vulnerabilities in third-party software are often targeted by attackers in the same way as vulnerabilities in the server's operating system, and neglecting to patch these components can leave the server exposed to exploits.

In large, complex environments, effective patch management requires collaboration between different teams within the organization. Security, IT, and development teams must work together to identify vulnerabilities, deploy patches, and monitor systems for potential issues. Regular communication between these teams ensures that all aspects of patch management are covered and that patches are applied in a timely and coordinated manner. The more efficiently these teams can collaborate, the faster vulnerabilities can be addressed and the better protected the server environment will be.

Regular patching and updates are fundamental to preventing exploits and securing server data. By addressing known vulnerabilities, improving performance, and ensuring the stability of the server environment, patch management plays a crucial role in maintaining a secure infrastructure. While patching can present challenges, such as the need for testing, downtime, and coordination, the benefits far outweigh the risks of leaving systems unpatched. By establishing a robust patching strategy, automating processes where possible, and regularly auditing the environment, organizations can significantly reduce the risk of exploits and ensure that their servers remain resilient to cyber threats.

Securing Server File Systems and Directories

One of the most critical aspects of securing a server is ensuring that its file systems and directories are properly protected. Servers host sensitive data, applications, and configurations that can be exploited if not adequately secured. The file system is where data is stored, managed, and accessed, and the security of this system is fundamental to the overall protection of a server. Without proper security measures in place, a compromised file system can allow unauthorized access to data, the installation of malicious software, or even a complete takeover of the server. Therefore, securing server file systems and directories involves implementing a series of best practices designed to reduce the attack surface and protect sensitive information from being accessed, altered, or deleted by unauthorized users.

The first step in securing a server's file system is to apply the principle of least privilege. This principle dictates that users and processes should only have the minimum level of access necessary to perform their required tasks. By limiting access to files and directories, organizations can significantly reduce the risk of accidental or intentional damage to the server's data. For example, users should only be granted read, write, or execute permissions for the specific files or directories they need to access. Any unnecessary permissions should be removed, ensuring that users cannot access data that is irrelevant to their role or responsibilities. This reduces the chance of malicious actors or compromised user accounts gaining unauthorized access to critical files.

Additionally, the use of file and directory permissions is essential to securing a server's file system. In most operating systems, such as Linux and Windows, administrators can set specific access controls on files and directories to define who can read, modify, or execute them. By configuring permissions carefully, administrators can ensure that sensitive files are only accessible to authorized users or system processes. For example, system configuration files, which control the behavior of the server and its applications, should only be accessible by the root user or administrators. This prevents regular users from modifying critical configurations that could impact the server's operation or security. Similarly, directories containing sensitive data, such as customer information or financial records, should be tightly secured to prevent unauthorized access. Regularly auditing file permissions is also a good practice to ensure that they remain in line with the principle of least privilege and that no excessive permissions have been granted.

Another important aspect of securing a server's file system is encrypting sensitive data. Encryption ensures that even if an attacker gains access to the server's file system, they will not be able to read the data without the appropriate decryption key. This is particularly important for files that contain personal information, financial data, or intellectual property. Disk-level encryption, which encrypts the entire file system or hard drive, provides strong protection for data at rest, ensuring that the data is secure even if the server is stolen or physically compromised. Additionally, file-level encryption can be applied to individual files or directories, allowing for more granular control over which data is encrypted. By implementing encryption, organizations can ensure that their data remains confidential, even in the event of a security breach.

In addition to encryption, securing the file system also involves protecting it from malware and unauthorized software installations. Servers are often targeted by malicious software, such as viruses, worms, or ransomware, which can exploit vulnerabilities in the file system to gain access or cause damage. One way to protect against this is by implementing file integrity monitoring tools. These tools track changes to files and directories, alerting administrators if unauthorized modifications are detected. For example, if an attacker gains access to the server and attempts to alter critical files, the file integrity monitoring system will identify the change and notify the administrator of a potential security breach. This allows for quick response and mitigation, reducing the potential damage caused by malicious software.

Another effective measure to protect the file system is to disable or limit the use of unnecessary services and applications that might introduce vulnerabilities. Many servers come with pre-installed software that may not be needed for the server's intended purpose. These unnecessary applications can increase the attack surface by potentially providing entry points for attackers. By reviewing the software installed on the server and removing any unnecessary applications or services, administrators can reduce the risk of compromise. For example, web servers should only have the necessary modules and extensions enabled, and database servers should only expose the required ports for communication. Minimizing the number of services running on a server also reduces the chances of vulnerabilities being exploited, thus securing the file system and its contents.

It is also essential to regularly back up critical files and directories to protect against data loss or corruption. While securing the file system from unauthorized access is vital, it is equally important to have a recovery plan in place in case of accidental deletion, hardware failure, or ransomware attacks. Regular backups ensure that organizations can quickly restore their systems to a known, secure state if something goes wrong. Backups should be encrypted to ensure that the data remains secure, even if the backup files are accessed by unauthorized individuals. Furthermore, backups should be stored in a secure location, such as an offsite or cloud-based storage service, to protect them from local threats like physical theft or fire.

An additional layer of protection for the server file system is the use of access control lists (ACLs). ACLs are more advanced than standard file permissions and allow administrators to define more granular access controls for specific files and directories. With ACLs, administrators can assign permissions to individual users or groups, specifying exactly what actions they can perform on a given file or directory. For instance, ACLs can be used to grant different levels of access to different departments within an organization, allowing employees to access only the files they need for their work while restricting access to sensitive data. By implementing ACLs, administrators can ensure that access to critical files is tightly controlled and that users do not have more access than necessary.

Monitoring file system activity is another critical component of securing server data. By continuously monitoring the file system, administrators can detect suspicious activity, such as attempts to access restricted files, execute unauthorized commands, or modify system files. File system monitoring tools can track file access patterns, log file modifications, and detect anomalies that may indicate a breach or malicious activity. These tools provide real-time alerts, allowing administrators to take immediate action if any suspicious activity is detected. In addition to monitoring file access, it is also essential to keep track of login attempts and user activity on the server to identify potential insider threats or compromised accounts.

Finally, securing server file systems and directories requires ongoing maintenance and regular security audits. As new vulnerabilities are discovered and threats evolve, it is crucial for administrators to stay informed and continuously assess the security of the file system. Regularly reviewing file permissions, auditing access logs, and testing encryption protocols help ensure that security measures remain effective. Additionally, administrators should apply patches and updates promptly to fix known vulnerabilities and maintain the integrity of the server's file system. By adopting a proactive approach to file system security, organizations can minimize the risk of unauthorized access and ensure that their data remains protected from cyber threats.

Securing server file systems and directories is a multifaceted process that requires careful planning, implementation, and ongoing vigilance. By applying the principle of least privilege, configuring file and directory permissions, encrypting sensitive data, and using additional security measures like file integrity monitoring and backup strategies, organizations can significantly reduce the risk of unauthorized access and data loss. Regular maintenance, audits, and monitoring further enhance the protection of the file system, ensuring that servers remain secure and resilient against emerging threats. Through these practices, organizations can safeguard their critical data and prevent malicious actors from exploiting weaknesses in the server's file system.

Hardening Web Servers: Best Practices for Apache and Nginx

Web servers are the backbone of the modern internet, hosting websites, applications, and services that millions of people access every day. Apache and Nginx are two of the most widely used web servers, both of which power a significant portion of the web today. However, with the increased frequency of cyberattacks, securing web servers has become more important than ever. These servers are prime targets for attackers who seek to exploit vulnerabilities in the server software, misconfigurations, or other weaknesses in the infrastructure. Hardening web servers such as Apache and Nginx involves implementing a series of best practices that enhance security and reduce the risk of unauthorized access, data breaches, and service disruptions.

The first step in hardening web servers is to minimize the number of unnecessary features and modules that are enabled. Both Apache and Nginx come with various modules that provide additional functionality but may also introduce vulnerabilities if not properly configured. For example, Apache includes modules for FTP, proxying, SSL, and more, but if these modules are not needed for the server's intended use, they should be disabled to reduce the attack surface. Similarly, Nginx comes with modules that enable reverse proxying, load balancing, and caching, but if these features are not required, they should be removed or kept inactive. Disabling unnecessary modules ensures that the server runs only the services it needs, reducing the risk of potential exploits in those modules.

Next, one of the most effective measures in securing Apache and Nginx servers is configuring proper access controls. This includes restricting access to sensitive parts of the server, such as configuration files, logs, and other system files. On Apache, directories such as /etc/httpd/ and /var/log/httpd/ contain sensitive configuration information and logs that should not be accessible to unauthorized users. Similarly, on Nginx, configuration files and logs must be protected from unauthorized access. Administrators should configure file permissions to ensure that only authorized users can access these critical files, and use tools such as chmod to set proper access rights. Additionally, web servers should be configured to prevent directory listing, ensuring that users cannot view the contents of directories that do not have an index file. This prevents attackers from discovering files that may be vulnerable or contain sensitive information.

One of the most important steps in web server hardening is configuring secure communication protocols. Both Apache and Nginx support SSL/TLS encryption, which secures communication between the server and clients by encrypting the data transmitted over the network. However, SSL/TLS must be configured properly to ensure that it provides adequate security. Administrators should disable old and vulnerable protocols, such as SSLv2 and SSLv3, and enforce the use of more secure protocols like TLS 1.2 or TLS 1.3. In addition, weak cipher suites should be disabled, and only strong, modern ciphers should be allowed to protect data during transmission. The use of HTTP Strict Transport Security (HSTS) should also be enforced, which tells browsers to only connect to the server over HTTPS, reducing the risk of man-in-the-middle attacks.

Another best practice for securing Apache and Nginx servers is implementing proper logging and monitoring. Logs provide valuable insight into server activity and can help identify potential security incidents, such as unauthorized access attempts or suspicious behavior. Both Apache and Nginx have robust logging features that can be configured to capture detailed information about incoming requests, error messages, and other server activities. Administrators should ensure that logs are stored in a secure location, with appropriate access controls in place, and set up centralized log management to simplify monitoring and analysis. Furthermore, logs should be regularly reviewed to detect any anomalies or security incidents, and automated monitoring tools can be set up to alert administrators to suspicious activity in real-time.

Securing the web server's operating system is another critical component of server hardening. The web server itself is often just one part of the overall server infrastructure, and the underlying operating system plays a significant role in securing the server. Both Apache and Nginx run on Linux, BSD, or Windows-based systems, and hardening the operating system is just as important as hardening the web server software. Administrators should ensure that the operating system is kept up to date with the latest patches and security updates, as unpatched systems are often the most vulnerable. This includes securing system configurations, disabling unnecessary services, and using firewalls to restrict access to the server. For example, a web server should not accept incoming connections from any IP address other than trusted sources, and unnecessary ports should be closed to minimize the number of potential attack vectors.

Configuring proper authentication is another essential part of securing web servers. On Apache, the mod_auth module can be used to implement password-based authentication for accessing certain directories or resources. Similarly, Nginx can be configured with basic authentication or integrate with other authentication methods, such as LDAP or OAuth, to control access to resources. Administrators should always ensure that authentication is used to protect sensitive areas of the server, such as the server's management interface or administrative tools. Password policies should also be enforced to ensure that strong passwords are used and regularly updated.

File and directory permissions also play a crucial role in securing web servers. Both Apache and Nginx run processes with specific user and group permissions, and it is essential to ensure that these permissions are set correctly to prevent unauthorized access to files. For example, the web server's user should only have access to the necessary directories, such as the document root, and not to other parts of the system that do not require access. By limiting the file system access of the web server's user, administrators can prevent potential exploitation by attackers who manage to gain access to the server. Additionally, the use of chroot jails or containerization techniques can further limit the impact of a potential breach by isolating the web server from the rest of the operating system.

Security headers are also an important aspect of securing web servers. HTTP headers can be used to provide additional security by instructing web browsers on how to handle requests and responses. Apache and Nginx both support a variety of security headers that can be configured to protect against common web vulnerabilities, such as Cross-Site Scripting (XSS) and Cross-Site Request Forgery (CSRF). For instance, the X-Content-Type-Options header can prevent browsers from interpreting files as a different MIME type, while the X-Frame-Options header can protect against clickjacking attacks by preventing the web page from being displayed in a frame or iframe. Configuring these headers correctly on both Apache and Nginx can add an additional layer of protection against web-based threats.

Finally, the server software itself should be kept up to date with the latest patches and security fixes. Both Apache and Nginx are actively maintained, and new versions are regularly released to address security vulnerabilities and improve functionality. Administrators should ensure that their servers are running the latest stable versions of Apache and Nginx, as older versions may contain known vulnerabilities that can be exploited by attackers. Regularly updating server software, as well as performing security audits and penetration testing, ensures that the server remains resilient against emerging threats and reduces the risk of successful exploitation.

Hardening web servers such as Apache and Nginx involves implementing a variety of best practices designed to enhance security and reduce vulnerabilities. Minimizing unnecessary modules, configuring secure communication protocols, enforcing proper access controls, and keeping the operating system and server software up to date are all critical steps in securing web servers. By following these best practices, administrators can ensure that their web servers are protected from common threats and are able to withstand attempts by cybercriminals to exploit weaknesses in the system. Securing Apache and Nginx servers requires a proactive approach to security, continual monitoring, and regular updates to maintain a secure environment.

Securing Databases: Strategies for MySQL, PostgreSQL, and More

Databases are at the heart of most applications and services, storing critical information that drives business operations. MySQL, PostgreSQL, and other database management systems are widely used due to their scalability, reliability, and ease of use. However, as valuable assets, databases are frequent targets for attackers who seek to exploit vulnerabilities to gain unauthorized access to sensitive data. Securing databases is an essential aspect of any organization's overall security strategy, as compromised databases can lead to data breaches, service disruptions, and significant reputational damage. To prevent these risks, it is important to follow best practices for securing database systems and protect them from both external and internal threats.

The first step in securing a database is to implement strong authentication mechanisms. Database access should be restricted to authorized users, and the authentication process should be robust to prevent unauthorized access. Both MySQL and PostgreSQL support user-based authentication, where each user is assigned a unique login and password. It is essential to configure these databases to require complex passwords for user accounts to mitigate the risk of brute-force attacks. Passwords should be long, complex, and contain a mixture of letters, numbers, and special characters. Additionally, multi-factor authentication (MFA) should be enabled where possible, particularly for database administrators and other high-privilege users, adding an extra layer of security by requiring more than just a password for authentication.

Another important aspect of securing databases is the principle of least privilege. Database users should only have access to the data and functions that are necessary for their roles. This means granting users the minimum level of access required for them to perform their tasks, whether they are querying data, performing updates, or managing configurations. For example, a user who only needs to read data should not be granted write or administrative permissions. Both MySQL and PostgreSQL support role-based access controls (RBAC) that allow administrators to create roles with specific permissions. Administrators can assign permissions to users based on their roles, ensuring that sensitive data is protected from unauthorized modifications and that users cannot perform actions that are beyond their scope of work. By restricting access to only the necessary parts of the database, organizations can minimize the risk of accidental or malicious actions that could compromise the database's integrity.

In addition to controlling access to the database, securing database connections is another critical step. Databases should be configured to enforce encrypted connections to prevent attackers from intercepting sensitive information during transmission. Both MySQL and PostgreSQL support SSL/TLS encryption for encrypting client-server communication, ensuring that data transmitted between the client and the server is protected from eavesdropping. Enabling SSL encryption ensures that even if an attacker intercepts the communication, they will not be able to read or modify the data. This is especially important when database servers are accessed over untrusted networks, such as the internet, as unencrypted connections can expose sensitive data to unauthorized parties. Administrators should also configure databases to reject connections from untrusted IP addresses, further reducing the chances of unauthorized access.

Another essential practice in securing databases is regularly updating and patching the database management system (DBMS). Like any software, MySQL, PostgreSQL, and other database systems can contain vulnerabilities that, if left unpatched, could be exploited by attackers. Vendors release security patches and updates to address known vulnerabilities, and it is crucial for administrators to stay up to date with these releases and apply patches as soon as they become available. Regular patching ensures that the database is protected from known threats, reducing the chances of a successful attack. In addition to applying security patches, administrators should also perform regular security audits to identify any misconfigurations or weaknesses in the database setup that could be exploited. These audits can help uncover potential vulnerabilities that may not have been addressed by standard patching practices.

Encryption is another critical tool for securing databases, especially when storing sensitive or personally identifiable information (PII). Both MySQL and PostgreSQL support encryption for data at rest, meaning that data stored in the database is encrypted when it is saved to disk. This ensures that if an attacker gains access to the physical storage, they will not be able to read the data without the proper decryption keys. Database encryption should be enabled to protect sensitive data, such as customer information, financial records, or health-related data. Additionally, encryption can be applied to individual columns or tables in the database, allowing administrators to encrypt only the most sensitive data while leaving other, less sensitive information unencrypted. This provides a balance between security and performance, ensuring that sensitive data remains protected while optimizing the overall performance of the database.

Database backups are another critical component of database security. Regular backups are essential for recovering from data loss or corruption caused by hardware failure, accidental deletion, or malicious attacks such as ransomware. However, backups themselves must also be secured to prevent unauthorized access. Backup files should be encrypted to ensure that the data remains protected even if the backup is stolen or accessed by an unauthorized party. Additionally, backups should be stored in a secure location, such as an offsite server or cloud storage, to protect them from local threats like fire or theft. It is also essential to test the backup and restore process regularly to ensure that backups can be restored in case of an emergency, and to verify that the data remains intact and uncorrupted.

Securing the physical and network environment in which the database resides is also essential. Databases should be deployed in a secure environment, such as a data center with restricted physical access. Database servers should be isolated from the rest of the network, with strict access controls preventing unauthorized users from accessing the server. Firewalls should be configured to limit inbound and outbound traffic to only trusted IP addresses, and intrusion detection systems (IDS) can be used to monitor network traffic for suspicious activity. Additionally, network segmentation can be employed to isolate database traffic from other parts of the network, further limiting the potential impact of a breach.

Audit logging is another important practice in securing databases. Both MySQL and PostgreSQL support detailed logging of database activity, including user logins, queries, and changes to the data. By enabling audit logging, administrators can track who accessed the database, what actions were taken, and whether any suspicious activity was detected. Regularly reviewing these logs can help administrators identify potential security incidents, such as unauthorized access or abnormal query patterns, and take corrective action before significant damage occurs. Logging can also provide valuable information for forensic analysis in the event of a security breach, helping organizations understand how the attack occurred and what steps can be taken to prevent similar incidents in the future.

Finally, it is essential to follow secure coding practices when developing database-driven applications. Applications that interact with databases should be designed to prevent common vulnerabilities, such as SQL injection attacks, which can be used to manipulate or retrieve data from the database. Prepared statements and parameterized queries should be used to prevent attackers from injecting malicious SQL code into the database. Additionally, applications should sanitize user inputs to ensure that only valid data is submitted to the database, and authentication and authorization mechanisms should be implemented to ensure that users only have access to the data they are authorized to view.

Securing databases is a multi-layered process that requires attention to detail and a comprehensive approach. By implementing strong authentication, encryption, access controls, and regular patching, organizations can significantly reduce the risk of unauthorized access and data breaches. Additionally, securing database backups, monitoring activity, and ensuring proper network and physical security are all critical components of a robust database security strategy. By following these best practices, organizations can ensure the integrity, confidentiality, and availability of their critical data, providing protection against both internal and external threats.

Configuring Intrusion Detection and Prevention Systems

In the world of network security, preventing unauthorized access and malicious activities is paramount to maintaining the integrity and confidentiality of sensitive data. Intrusion Detection and Prevention Systems (IDPS) are essential components of a comprehensive security strategy. These systems are designed to detect and respond to potential security threats in real time, helping organizations identify and mitigate attacks before they cause significant damage. Intrusion detection systems (IDS) passively monitor network traffic for suspicious activity, while intrusion prevention systems (IPS) take a more proactive approach, actively blocking or mitigating potential threats. Properly configuring and maintaining these systems is crucial to ensuring they provide maximum protection against cyber threats.

The first step in configuring an IDPS is determining the type of system that best suits the organization's needs. There are two main types of IDPS: network-based and host-based. A network-based intrusion detection system (NIDS) monitors network traffic, looking for signs of malicious activity such as unusual traffic patterns, unauthorized access attempts, or known attack signatures. NIDS are typically deployed at strategic points in the network, such as at the perimeter or in front of critical servers, to monitor traffic entering or leaving the network. On the other hand, a host-based intrusion detection system (HIDS) is installed on individual servers or endpoints to monitor the activity of those systems, such as file access, user actions, and system logs. The choice between NIDS and HIDS depends on the organization's network architecture and the type of traffic or systems that need to be protected.

Once the appropriate type of IDPS has been selected, configuring the system involves setting up the monitoring parameters and defining what constitutes suspicious activity. The most basic configuration involves defining attack signatures, which are predefined patterns that represent known attacks or vulnerabilities. These signatures can be based on common methods of attack, such as SQL injection, cross-site scripting (XSS), or denial of service (DoS) attacks. The system will compare incoming network traffic or system activity against these signatures, alerting administrators if a match is found. While signature-based detection is effective at identifying known threats, it can be less effective against new or unknown attacks, which is why many modern IDPS systems also incorporate anomaly-based detection.

Anomaly-based detection works by establishing a baseline of normal network or system behavior and then identifying deviations from that baseline. This type of detection can help identify new or zero-day attacks that do not have known signatures. For example, if a server suddenly begins sending large amounts of traffic to an unfamiliar destination or if a user attempts to access a large number of files in a short period, an anomaly-based IDPS may flag this behavior as suspicious. However, anomaly-based detection can also result in false positives, especially if the baseline is not accurately defined. Fine-tuning the parameters of the system and continually reviewing the alerts generated by the IDPS is essential to minimize these false positives and ensure that the system provides accurate and actionable alerts.

Once the detection system is configured, the next step is to integrate the IDPS with other security systems in the organization's infrastructure. For instance, IDPS can be integrated with firewalls, anti-virus software, and Security Information and Event Management (SIEM) systems. Firewalls can work in tandem with IDPS by blocking traffic based on rules defined by the detection system. If the IDPS detects an attack signature or anomaly, it can trigger the firewall to block the malicious traffic or restrict access to the targeted system. Similarly, SIEM systems can collect and analyze logs generated by the IDPS and other security devices, providing a centralized view of security events and helping to identify trends or patterns in the data. Integrating the IDPS with other security systems helps create a layered defense strategy, ensuring that multiple layers of security work together to detect, prevent, and respond to attacks.

For organizations that need real-time protection against ongoing attacks, an intrusion prevention system (IPS) may be necessary. While IDS systems simply monitor traffic and alert administrators to potential threats, IPS systems take a more proactive approach by blocking malicious traffic or actions before they can cause harm. IPS systems can block incoming traffic that matches attack signatures or that deviates significantly from the established baseline. For example, if the IPS detects an attempt to exploit a known vulnerability in a web application, it can block the request before it reaches the server. Some IPS systems also allow for customized rule creation, enabling organizations to create specific rules tailored to their network environment and business needs. This flexibility is crucial in blocking emerging threats and ensuring that the IPS can adapt to new attack techniques.

To maximize the effectiveness of an IDPS, it is essential to fine-tune the system regularly. This involves reviewing and adjusting the detection rules, updating signatures to account for new attack methods, and ensuring that the system is operating at peak performance. Because cyber threats evolve constantly, IDPS systems must be continuously updated to stay ahead of attackers. This includes applying updates from vendors, adding new signatures to the detection database, and adjusting thresholds for anomaly detection. Failure to update and fine-tune the IDPS can lead to missed threats, false positives, or unnecessary alerts that overwhelm administrators and reduce the system's effectiveness. Regularly testing the IDPS with simulated attacks, such as penetration testing or red teaming, can also help identify any gaps in coverage or areas that need improvement.

Another important consideration when configuring an IDPS is the management of alerts and responses. An IDPS generates a large volume of alerts, many of which may be false positives or low-priority events. To avoid alert fatigue and ensure that critical threats are addressed, administrators need to define a clear process for prioritizing and responding to alerts. This process may involve setting up different severity levels for alerts, categorizing events based on the potential impact, and defining clear procedures for investigating and mitigating threats. Automated response actions, such as blocking IP addresses or shutting down specific ports, can be configured for high-severity alerts, enabling the system to take immediate action in the event of an attack. However, it is important to ensure that these automated responses do not interfere with legitimate traffic or disrupt normal business operations.

One challenge in configuring an IDPS is the balance between security and performance. While an IDPS provides critical security benefits, it can also introduce overhead that impacts network or system performance. Network-based IDPS, in particular, can become a bottleneck if not properly optimized, as they must inspect large volumes of traffic in real time. To address this, administrators should configure the IDPS to prioritize traffic based on the organization's needs, ensuring that critical systems and applications receive the attention they require. This may involve segmenting the network, adjusting monitoring parameters, or offloading some of the detection tasks to specialized hardware or cloud-based solutions. Properly sizing the IDPS and ensuring that it can handle the network's traffic volume without causing delays is crucial for maintaining optimal performance.

Finally, it is essential to regularly review and update the IDPS configuration as part of the organization's broader security strategy. As the network evolves, new devices, applications, and users are added, and the threat landscape changes. An IDPS that is not regularly updated may miss emerging threats or fail to account for new vulnerabilities in the network. Administrators should schedule periodic reviews of the IDPS configuration, test the system's performance, and adjust detection rules and response actions to keep pace with the changing network environment. Collaboration with other security teams and the use of threat intelligence feeds can also help ensure that the IDPS remains aligned with the latest security trends and threats.

Configuring an Intrusion Detection and Prevention System is a dynamic and ongoing process that requires careful planning, regular updates, and fine-tuning. By properly setting up the system to monitor network traffic and system activity, integrating it with other security systems, and ensuring that it is regularly updated and optimized, organizations can significantly enhance their ability to detect, prevent, and respond to potential security threats. The proactive nature of an IDPS allows organizations to mitigate risks before they result in significant damage, helping to safeguard critical assets and maintain a secure network environment.

Monitoring Server Activity for Early Detection of Threats

In an era where cyberattacks are becoming increasingly sophisticated, monitoring server activity is crucial for identifying potential threats before they escalate into significant breaches or disruptions. Servers are often at the heart of an organization's digital infrastructure, hosting sensitive data and critical applications. As such, they are frequent targets for cybercriminals, insiders, and automated attack tools that attempt to exploit vulnerabilities. The ability to detect these threats early can mean the difference between a minor incident and a catastrophic data breach. Monitoring server activity is an essential strategy for early threat detection, as it provides real-time visibility into system behavior, network traffic, and user actions, enabling administrators to respond quickly and mitigate risks.

At the core of monitoring server activity is the collection and analysis of log data generated by the server and its associated services. Every action performed on a server, from login attempts to file access, is recorded in logs. These logs provide a detailed account of server activity, and when analyzed properly, they can help identify irregularities, suspicious behavior, or signs of an ongoing attack. For example, a sudden spike in login attempts from a particular IP address could signal a brute-force attack, while unusual system resource usage might indicate a denial of service (DoS) attempt. By continuously monitoring these logs, administrators can spot these indicators of compromise (IOCs) early on and take appropriate action to prevent further damage. Log monitoring tools, such as Security Information and Event Management (SIEM) systems, can be used to aggregate and analyze log data from multiple sources, providing a centralized view of server activity and improving the chances of detecting potential threats.

While log monitoring is a key component, it is also essential to monitor server performance and system health. Unusual behavior in system performance often signals that something is wrong, whether it's a potential security threat or a system malfunction. For example, high CPU usage or memory consumption might suggest that a server is being overwhelmed by an attacker conducting a DoS attack, or it could indicate the presence of malware running on the system. Similarly, slow response times or unexpected system reboots may point to an underlying issue that could be related to a security breach, such as a compromised process attempting to hide its activities. By continuously monitoring server health metrics and resource utilization, administrators can identify and respond to performance anomalies before they lead to more significant issues. Monitoring tools can track system metrics such as CPU usage, disk space, memory usage, network throughput, and process activity, providing administrators with a comprehensive overview of the server's state.

User activity is another critical area to monitor for early threat detection. Servers are often accessed by multiple users, including administrators, employees, and external clients. Monitoring user activity is essential for detecting signs of malicious or unauthorized behavior. This can include tracking login attempts, file access, and command execution. For example, an administrator who accesses files or systems they do not normally interact with might indicate that their account has been compromised. Similarly, a regular user who suddenly begins accessing sensitive directories or executing administrative commands may be an indicator of suspicious activity. By setting up alerts for abnormal user behavior, administrators can quickly detect potential insider threats or compromised accounts. Monitoring user activity also helps ensure that the principle of least privilege is being followed, as it allows administrators to see whether users are accessing only the resources necessary for their role.

Another essential component of server activity monitoring is network traffic analysis. A significant portion of cyberattacks is carried out through network-based methods, such as SQL injections, cross-site scripting (XSS), or malware downloads. Monitoring network traffic allows administrators to detect signs of malicious communication between the server and external entities. This includes looking for unusual outbound traffic, such as large volumes of data being transferred to an external IP address, which could indicate a data exfiltration attempt. Similarly, incoming traffic spikes or traffic from suspicious locations could signal an attempted attack, such as a DDoS or a port scan designed to identify vulnerabilities. Analyzing network traffic and correlating it with other server activity can help identify attacks in their early stages, enabling a quick response to block malicious communication and protect the server.

Intrusion detection systems (IDS) and intrusion prevention systems (IPS) are also critical tools in the server monitoring arsenal. These systems are designed to detect and, in the case of IPS, prevent unauthorized access and malicious activity. IDS systems monitor network traffic and system activity for known attack signatures or anomalous behavior, such as a user attempting to execute a command outside their typical behavior. When suspicious activity is detected, the IDS can generate alerts, allowing administrators to investigate further. An IPS takes this a step further by actively blocking malicious traffic or actions in real-time, preventing an attack from progressing before it causes harm. These systems can be configured to detect a wide range of attacks, including brute-force attempts, unauthorized access, and exploitation of known vulnerabilities. By integrating IDS/IPS with other monitoring tools, administrators can create a layered defense against attacks, allowing for both detection and prevention of malicious activity.

Early detection of threats is not only about identifying malicious activity but also about understanding the context of that activity. Administrators must be able to distinguish between false positives and genuine threats. This requires configuring monitoring tools to take into account the normal behavior of the server and its users. For example, an increase in login attempts during regular maintenance hours may not be suspicious, but the same behavior at odd hours might raise a red flag. Machine learning algorithms and behavior-based analytics can be used to improve the accuracy of threat detection by learning what constitutes normal activity and flagging deviations from that norm. As the monitoring system learns over time, it can become more adept at distinguishing between routine activities and potentially malicious behavior, reducing the volume of false alerts and ensuring that administrators can focus on genuine threats.

Alerting and response mechanisms are equally important when monitoring server activity for early detection. Alerts are essential for informing administrators of suspicious activity, but the effectiveness of these alerts depends on their configuration. Administrators should ensure that alerts are prioritized based on severity, with high-priority events triggering immediate attention and low-priority events being monitored over time. Alerts should also include sufficient context to allow administrators to quickly understand the nature of the threat and the potential impact. For example, an alert that indicates a failed login attempt should include information about the source IP address, the username used, and the time of the attempt, helping administrators to determine whether it's a legitimate attempt or part of a brute-force attack.

In addition to alerts, automated response actions can be configured to mitigate the impact of threats. For example, if an IDS detects a potential attack, it can trigger an automatic response to block the source IP address or isolate the affected system from the network. These automated responses help contain the threat and reduce the time between detection and mitigation, minimizing the potential damage caused by an attack.

Regularly reviewing server activity and continuously refining monitoring configurations is necessary to adapt to the evolving nature of cyber threats. As new vulnerabilities and attack methods emerge, the monitoring system must be updated to detect and respond to these changes. Regular vulnerability assessments, penetration testing, and threat intelligence sharing are vital components of a proactive monitoring strategy, ensuring that the system remains responsive to the latest threats. Moreover, a well-structured incident response plan should be in place to guide administrators in the event of a detected threat, ensuring that appropriate actions are taken quickly and efficiently to minimize damage.

Effective server activity monitoring provides critical insight into the health and security of the server environment. By continuously tracking user behavior, system performance, network traffic, and other activities, administrators can detect threats early, enabling timely responses that can prevent data breaches, system compromises, and other security incidents.

Implementing Effective Backup and Recovery Strategies

In the digital age, data is one of the most valuable assets for any organization. It is the foundation of business operations, decision-making, and long-term planning. However, despite the growing reliance on digital systems, organizations face the constant risk of data loss due to unforeseen events, such as hardware failures, software malfunctions, human error, or even cyberattacks. To protect against these risks, organizations must implement effective backup and recovery strategies. A comprehensive backup and recovery plan ensures that critical data can be restored quickly and accurately in the event of an incident, minimizing downtime and reducing the impact of data loss.

The first key consideration when implementing a backup strategy is determining what data needs to be backed up. Not all data within an organization is equally important. For example, some data may be critical for daily operations, while other data may be less essential. Identifying and classifying data based on its importance helps organizations prioritize their backup efforts. Mission-critical systems, databases, and files that are essential for the business to function should be given the highest priority. Non-essential data or data that can be easily reconstructed, such as temporary files or cached data, can be excluded from regular backups. The backup process should focus on ensuring that the most important data is securely backed up and can be recovered quickly in the event of an incident.

Once the data to be backed up has been identified, the next step is to decide on the frequency of backups. The frequency of backups depends on the nature of the data and how often it changes. For example, a database that is updated frequently, such as an e-commerce system, will need to be backed up more frequently than a system that is less active. Backup strategies typically include a combination of full, incremental, and differential backups. A full backup involves copying all the data in the system, while incremental backups only copy data that has changed since the last backup, and differential backups copy data that has changed since the last full backup. Full backups provide a complete snapshot of the system, but they require more storage space and time to complete. Incremental and differential backups are more efficient in terms of storage and time, as they only capture changes made since the last backup. A combination of these backup types can be used to balance data protection with efficiency.

An effective backup strategy also requires choosing the right storage medium for the backups. There are several options available for storing backups, each with its own advantages and disadvantages. On-premises backups, stored on physical devices such as hard drives or network-attached storage (NAS), provide quick access to backup data but may be vulnerable to physical damage, theft, or disaster. Offsite backups, such as those stored in remote data centers, provide an added layer of protection by ensuring that backup data is not affected by local disasters like fires, floods, or theft. Cloud backups are becoming increasingly popular due to their scalability, flexibility, and remote access capabilities. Cloud providers offer secure, redundant storage solutions that can automatically scale as backup data grows. Cloud backups also offer the advantage of being accessible from anywhere, making them a convenient option for organizations with distributed teams or multiple locations.

Another crucial consideration when implementing backup strategies is data encryption. Data stored in backups is often sensitive and must be protected to prevent unauthorized access. Encryption ensures that even if backup data is intercepted or stolen, it remains unreadable to unauthorized users. Backup data should be encrypted both in transit, as it is being transferred to the backup storage, and at rest, while it is stored on the backup medium. Encryption keys should be securely managed, and access to encrypted data should be restricted to authorized personnel only. This helps ensure the confidentiality and integrity of backup data, providing an additional layer of protection against cyberattacks and data breaches.

Testing backup and recovery procedures is an often-overlooked yet critical aspect of an effective backup strategy. Backups are only valuable if they can be reliably restored when needed. Regularly testing backup systems ensures that the data can be recovered quickly and accurately in the event of a disaster. Testing should be done periodically to verify the integrity of the backups, confirm that the recovery process works as expected, and assess the time it takes to restore the data. It is important to test both the restoration of individual files and the recovery of entire systems to ensure that all critical data can be restored. By performing regular recovery drills, organizations can identify any gaps or issues in their backup process and address them before a real incident occurs.

The recovery process itself must be carefully planned and documented to ensure that it is efficient and effective when the need arises. A detailed recovery plan outlines the steps that should be taken to restore data, systems, and applications, as well as the personnel responsible for executing these steps. The plan should include clear instructions on how to recover from different types of incidents, such as a ransomware attack, a hardware failure, or a natural disaster. Key personnel should be trained in the recovery process, and the plan should be regularly reviewed and updated to reflect changes in the organization's infrastructure and data. A well-documented and practiced recovery plan ensures that the organization can respond quickly and effectively to data loss incidents, minimizing downtime and reducing the impact on business operations.

Additionally, organizations should consider implementing automated backup solutions that streamline the backup process and reduce the risk of human error. Automated backup systems can be configured to run at regular intervals, ensuring that backups are consistently performed without the need for manual intervention. These systems can also send notifications to administrators if a backup fails, allowing them to address any issues promptly. Automation helps reduce the administrative burden associated with manual backups, ensuring that critical data is always protected and that backups are completed on schedule.

As part of the overall backup strategy, organizations should also develop a retention policy that dictates how long backup data should be stored. Not all backup data needs to be kept indefinitely. A well-defined retention policy helps organizations manage storage resources and ensure that only the necessary backup data is retained. For example, organizations may choose to retain daily backups for the past week, weekly backups for the past month, and monthly backups for the past year. This ensures that the organization has sufficient historical data available to recover from various types of incidents while managing storage space efficiently.

Finally, organizations must remain vigilant in monitoring their backup systems to ensure that they are functioning correctly. Monitoring tools can alert administrators if a backup fails, if storage capacity is running low, or if there are any issues with the backup process. Proactive monitoring helps identify and address potential problems before they impact the organization's ability to recover data in the event of an incident.

Implementing effective backup and recovery strategies is essential for safeguarding critical data and minimizing the impact of data loss. By determining what data to back up, selecting appropriate backup frequencies and storage mediums, encrypting backup data, and regularly testing recovery processes, organizations can ensure that they are well-prepared for potential disruptions. Automated systems, well-documented recovery plans, and proactive monitoring further enhance the reliability and efficiency of backup systems. These practices provide organizations with the peace of mind that they can quickly recover their critical data, ensuring business continuity and protecting against the growing threat of data loss.

Protecting Against Distributed Denial of Service (DDoS) Attacks

In an increasingly interconnected world, the threat of Distributed Denial of Service (DDoS) attacks looms large over organizations and individuals alike. These attacks are among the most common and disruptive cyber threats, capable of causing widespread service outages, financial losses, and reputational damage. A DDoS attack occurs when multiple systems, often compromised devices controlled by attackers, are used to flood a targeted server or network with an overwhelming amount of traffic. This excessive load can cripple the targeted system, making it unavailable to legitimate users and causing significant downtime. Given the potential damage that DDoS attacks can inflict, it is crucial for organizations to understand how these attacks work and implement effective strategies for mitigating their impact.

The nature of a DDoS attack is that it relies on a large volume of traffic coming from various sources. Unlike a traditional DoS (Denial of Service) attack, where a single machine or network is used to launch the attack, a DDoS attack uses a distributed network of compromised systems. These systems, which may include infected computers, IoT devices, or other networked devices, work together under the control of a cybercriminal to send traffic to the target. The traffic typically consists of requests, which, when combined in large numbers, can overwhelm the target system, consuming its resources such as bandwidth, CPU, or memory, and rendering it unresponsive. DDoS attacks are often carried out using botnets—large networks of infected devices controlled remotely by the attacker. These botnets can generate vast amounts of traffic that are difficult to block due to the sheer scale and distribution of the attack.

The first step in protecting against DDoS attacks is to understand the threat landscape and assess the risk to your organization. Every organization's exposure to DDoS attacks will vary depending on factors such as the size of the organization, its digital presence, and the type of services it offers. For example, e-commerce sites, financial institutions, and gaming platforms are often targeted by DDoS attacks due to their reliance on uptime and the financial or reputational damage that downtime can cause. An assessment should identify the most critical assets and services that need to be protected and help define the organization's risk tolerance. Once these areas are identified, specific DDoS mitigation strategies can be tailored to address the unique vulnerabilities and needs of the organization.

One of the most effective defenses against DDoS attacks is the use of rate limiting. Rate limiting involves setting thresholds for the number of requests that a server will accept from a particular IP address or system within a specific time frame. By limiting the rate at which requests can be made, the server can prevent itself from becoming overwhelmed by an excessive number of requests. This strategy can help mitigate smaller-scale DDoS attacks, particularly those that target specific applications or web services. However, rate limiting is often not sufficient for large-scale DDoS attacks, where traffic comes from many different sources. In such cases, additional layers of protection are required.

Another effective defense is to use a content delivery network (CDN). CDNs are networks of distributed servers that cache and deliver content to users based on their geographic location. By distributing traffic across multiple servers, a CDN can help absorb the load of a DDoS attack and reduce the strain on the primary server. CDNs typically have large-scale infrastructures that are capable of handling significant traffic volumes, which makes them particularly useful for mitigating DDoS attacks. Many CDN providers also offer DDoS protection services as part of their infrastructure, utilizing advanced traffic filtering techniques to detect and block malicious traffic before it reaches the origin server. Leveraging a CDN not only helps protect against DDoS attacks but also improves the overall performance of web services by reducing latency and increasing speed.

In addition to using CDNs, organizations should implement cloud-based DDoS protection services. Many cloud service providers, such as AWS, Azure, and Google Cloud, offer DDoS protection services that are designed to scale automatically in response to large attacks. These cloud-based services leverage the vast resources of the cloud to absorb and mitigate DDoS traffic, ensuring that the target server remains operational even during an attack. Cloud-based DDoS protection typically uses a combination of techniques, including traffic analysis, IP reputation filtering, and behavior-based detection, to identify and block malicious traffic in real-time. This type of protection is particularly useful for organizations that may not have the infrastructure or resources to handle a large-scale DDoS attack on their own.

Network firewalls and intrusion prevention systems (IPS) can also play a role in defending against DDoS attacks. Firewalls can be configured to detect and block traffic from suspicious IP addresses or networks, while intrusion prevention systems can analyze incoming traffic for signs of attack patterns, such as unusually high traffic volumes or malformed packets. By configuring these security devices to specifically look for DDoS-related traffic, organizations can block a significant portion of malicious requests before they reach the server. However, firewalls and IPS devices may struggle to effectively mitigate large-scale DDoS attacks, especially when the volume of traffic is overwhelming. This is why they are typically used as part of a multi-layered defense strategy, alongside other DDoS mitigation tools.

One of the challenges with DDoS attacks is that they can often be difficult to distinguish from legitimate traffic, particularly in large-scale attacks that involve sophisticated techniques like IP spoofing or amplification. To address this challenge, many organizations deploy traffic anomaly detection systems. These systems use machine learning algorithms and behavioral analytics to analyze network traffic in real time, looking for deviations from typical usage patterns. For example, if a website experiences a sudden surge in traffic from previously unknown IP addresses, the traffic anomaly detection system can raise an alert and trigger a response. These systems are valuable for detecting DDoS attacks in their early stages, enabling organizations to implement mitigation measures before the attack escalates.

While technical measures are essential for defending against DDoS attacks, it is equally important for organizations to have a well-defined incident response plan in place. In the event of an attack, the organization needs to be able to respond quickly and efficiently. The response plan should outline clear procedures for identifying and mitigating DDoS attacks, including steps for escalating the issue to the appropriate teams, contacting service providers or DDoS mitigation services, and communicating with stakeholders. Regular drills should be conducted to ensure that all team members are familiar with the procedures and that the response plan is effective in minimizing downtime and damage.

Collaboration with your internet service provider (ISP) can also play a crucial role in defending against DDoS attacks. Many ISPs offer DDoS protection services that are designed to help mitigate attacks before they reach the organization's network. These services typically involve traffic filtering, blackholing, or redirecting traffic to scrubbing centers where malicious traffic can be filtered out. By working closely with the ISP, organizations can ensure that they have additional layers of protection in place and that they can quickly escalate the issue to the right personnel when an attack is detected.

DDoS attacks continue to be a significant threat to organizations of all sizes, but with a comprehensive strategy in place, it is possible to mitigate their impact. By implementing a combination of rate limiting, CDNs, cloud-based DDoS protection, firewalls, IPS, anomaly detection, and strong incident response plans, organizations can reduce the likelihood of a successful attack and ensure that they can maintain service availability in the face of a DDoS threat. Proactive preparation and continuous monitoring are key to minimizing the risks posed by these attacks and ensuring that business operations remain secure and uninterrupted.

The Importance of System Logging and Log Management

In the realm of cybersecurity and systems administration, system logging and log management are among the most critical practices for ensuring the integrity, security, and operational efficiency of an IT infrastructure. Logs provide a comprehensive, real-time record of system activities, user actions, and network traffic, which serve as an invaluable resource for monitoring, troubleshooting, auditing, and identifying potential security incidents. Without proper system logging and log management practices, organizations risk missing crucial indicators of malicious activities, system failures, or unauthorized access, which can lead to prolonged downtime, data breaches, or significant financial losses. Therefore, understanding the importance of logging and the methods for managing logs is essential for maintaining a secure and efficient system environment.

System logging is the process of recording events, actions, and processes that occur within a system. These logs can be generated by various sources, such as the operating system, applications, network devices, and security systems. Logs capture detailed information about system operations, including errors, successful and failed login attempts, network connections, and application errors. This data, when properly collected and analyzed, can offer insight into the health of the system, the behavior of users, and the activities of potential attackers. For instance, logs can help identify unusual patterns, such as a high number of failed login attempts or access to unauthorized resources, which may indicate a brute-force attack or an insider threat. Logs are also crucial for tracing the actions leading up to a security breach, providing forensic evidence to understand how the attack occurred and what data or systems were compromised.

One of the most significant benefits of system logging is the ability to detect and respond to security threats in a timely manner. Modern cyber threats, including malware, ransomware, and advanced persistent threats (APTs), often operate under the radar and can remain undetected for extended periods. System logs offer the first line of defense by capturing events that may be associated with these threats. For example, logs can reveal when a system is communicating with known malicious IP addresses or when there is an unexpected increase in network traffic that could signify a Distributed Denial of Service (DDoS) attack. By continuously monitoring these logs, administrators can identify suspicious activity early and take preventive measures to mitigate the impact of an attack. In this way, logging provides a proactive security measure that helps organizations stay ahead of potential threats.

In addition to threat detection, system logs are invaluable for troubleshooting and maintaining system performance. They provide administrators with detailed records of system events, which can be used to diagnose issues and identify the root causes of system failures. Whether a server is experiencing performance degradation, an application is crashing, or a network device is malfunctioning, logs offer critical insights that can help resolve these problems quickly and efficiently. By analyzing log data, administrators can identify patterns that indicate the source of the issue, such as software bugs, configuration errors, or hardware failures. Without effective log management, administrators would be forced to rely on trial and error or incomplete information to resolve issues, leading to increased downtime and operational inefficiency.

Log management, however, is not simply about collecting logs; it is about effectively storing, organizing, and analyzing the data to extract meaningful insights. Logs can generate vast amounts of data, especially in large environments with numerous systems and devices. Managing this data becomes increasingly challenging as the volume grows, and without proper management practices, it can become overwhelming and difficult to navigate. Log management tools are essential for aggregating logs from multiple sources, normalizing the data, and making it accessible for analysis. These tools often include search and filtering capabilities, which allow administrators to quickly locate specific events or patterns within the logs. Additionally, log management solutions can automate the process of categorizing and prioritizing log data, enabling administrators to focus on the most critical issues. Effective log management ensures that logs are not just stored but are actively utilized to improve system security and performance.

A crucial aspect of log management is ensuring that logs are retained for an appropriate amount of time. Logs can provide valuable historical data for auditing purposes and for understanding trends in system activity over time. For instance, logs can help organizations track user behavior, monitor system changes, and identify compliance issues. In regulated industries, retaining logs for a certain period is often a legal requirement. However, storing logs indefinitely is not practical due to storage limitations and the volume of data generated. A log retention policy should be established to ensure that logs are kept for an adequate duration, based on legal, regulatory, and operational needs. At the same time, older logs should be archived or deleted to prevent storage systems from becoming overloaded, while ensuring that critical logs are preserved for future reference.

Log security is another important consideration in log management. Logs contain sensitive information, such as system configurations, user actions, and access credentials, which could be exploited if they fall into the wrong hands. To prevent unauthorized access, logs should be stored in secure, access-controlled environments. This means restricting access to logs to only authorized personnel who need the information to perform their duties. Furthermore, logs should be encrypted to protect their confidentiality and integrity, especially when transmitted over the network or stored in remote locations. Without these security measures, logs themselves can become a target for attackers seeking to gain insights into system vulnerabilities or to cover their tracks after a breach.

A robust logging strategy also includes the regular auditing of log data. Audit trails provide a comprehensive history of system activity, and reviewing them regularly helps ensure that security policies are being followed and that no unauthorized actions are taking place. For example, by auditing logs, administrators can verify that users are not accessing sensitive data without permission or that configurations are not being changed without proper authorization. Regular audits can also help ensure compliance with industry regulations and standards, such as GDPR, HIPAA, or PCI DSS, which often require specific logging practices to be in place. By proactively auditing logs, organizations can identify and address issues before they lead to more serious security incidents.

Furthermore, integration with other security systems enhances the effectiveness of logging and log management. When logs are integrated with tools like Security Information and Event Management (SIEM) systems, intrusion detection systems (IDS), or intrusion prevention systems (IPS), the organization benefits from a more comprehensive view of its security posture. SIEM systems, for example, aggregate log data from multiple sources, analyze it for suspicious activity, and generate alerts when potential threats are detected. This integration allows for faster response times and more informed decision-making when an incident occurs. In addition, the correlation of log data from different systems helps identify complex, multi-stage attacks that might otherwise go unnoticed.

In large or complex environments, automation plays a critical role in managing logs efficiently. Automated systems can help streamline the process of log collection, storage, analysis, and alerting, reducing the burden on administrators and ensuring that potential threats are detected and addressed in real time. Automated log monitoring can be configured to generate alerts for specific events, such as failed login attempts, privilege escalation, or abnormal system behavior. By automating routine tasks, organizations can ensure that log data is continuously monitored, analyzed, and acted upon, allowing for a more effective and timely response to security incidents.

System logging and log management are foundational to maintaining the security, performance, and compliance of an organization's IT infrastructure. By capturing and analyzing system activity, logs provide critical insights into the health of the system and the behavior of users, enabling administrators to detect and respond to threats before they escalate. Effective log management ensures that logs are organized, secure, and retained for the appropriate amount of time, while regular auditing and integration with other security systems enhance the overall effectiveness of the strategy. By implementing a comprehensive logging and log management strategy, organizations can better protect their systems, detect potential threats early, and ensure the integrity of their data and operations.

Hardening SSH for Secure Remote Administration

Secure Shell (SSH) is a widely used protocol for remote administration and secure communication between systems. It provides an encrypted channel for managing servers, transferring files, and executing commands remotely, ensuring that sensitive data, such as login credentials and commands, remain protected during transmission. However, the widespread use of SSH makes it a prime target for attackers, who often exploit weak configurations or default settings to gain unauthorized access. Hardening SSH is a critical step in securing servers and ensuring that remote administration remains safe from unauthorized access, brute-force attacks, and other threats. By implementing best practices for SSH configuration and regularly reviewing settings, organizations can significantly enhance the security of their remote administration processes.

The first step in hardening SSH is to configure the server to use only secure encryption algorithms. SSH supports a variety of cryptographic algorithms that define how the data is encrypted during communication. By default, SSH may enable older, less secure algorithms that are vulnerable to attacks. For example, older ciphers like DES and 3DES have been found to be susceptible to various cryptographic attacks and should be disabled. Instead, modern, stronger ciphers such as AES (Advanced Encryption Standard) and ChaCha20 should be used, as they provide much stronger security for data transmission. Additionally, administrators should ensure that SSH is configured to use secure key exchange algorithms, such as ECDHE (Elliptic Curve Diffie-Hellman Ephemeral), which offer a higher level of security and forward secrecy.

Another essential step in hardening SSH is disabling root login. By default, the root user has full administrative access to the server, making it a highly desirable target for attackers. Allowing root login via SSH presents a significant security risk, as attackers only need to crack the root password or exploit a vulnerability to gain complete control of the system. To mitigate this risk, administrators should disable root login over SSH and instead use a regular user account with elevated privileges. This can be accomplished by modifying the SSH configuration file to prevent root login, which forces administrators to authenticate as a regular user and then use sudo or similar tools to escalate privileges when needed. This extra layer of security reduces the likelihood of attackers gaining full control of the system.

Additionally, SSH access should be restricted to specific users and groups. By default, SSH allows any user with a valid account on the system to attempt a login, which can be problematic if there are many users with remote access privileges. Restricting SSH access to a limited set of users and groups ensures that only authorized individuals can log in to the server remotely. Administrators can configure the AllowUsers or AllowGroups directives in the SSH configuration file to specify which users or groups are permitted to access the system via SSH. This simple step can drastically reduce the number of potential entry points for attackers, as it limits the scope of who can attempt to authenticate.

One of the most effective methods for securing SSH access is by using public key authentication rather than password-based authentication. Password-based authentication is vulnerable to brute-force attacks, where attackers repeatedly guess passwords until they find the correct one. In contrast, public key authentication uses a cryptographic key pair: a public key stored on the server and a private key held securely by the user. This method provides a much higher level of security because the private key is never transmitted over the network, making it virtually impossible for attackers to intercept or steal it. Administrators should configure SSH to only allow public key authentication and disable password-based logins by setting the PasswordAuthentication directive to "no" in the SSH configuration file. This ensures that only users with the correct private key can access the server, making it significantly harder for attackers to gain unauthorized access.

Another important aspect of SSH hardening is the implementation of rate limiting and intrusion detection mechanisms to prevent brute-force attacks. Brute-force attacks involve attempting to guess the password by trying a large number of possible combinations. These attacks can be automated using specialized tools, and if not detected and mitigated, they can eventually lead to successful unauthorized access. One of the most effective ways to combat brute-force attacks is by implementing rate limiting, which restricts the number of login attempts from a particular IP address within a specified time period. This can be achieved using tools such as fail2ban, which automatically detects and blocks IP addresses that make too many failed login attempts. By setting up rate limiting and banning policies, administrators can significantly reduce the risk of brute-force attacks and prevent attackers from overwhelming the system with login attempts.

In addition to rate limiting, SSH hardening should include logging and monitoring SSH access attempts. Monitoring is crucial for identifying and responding to suspicious activity quickly. By enabling detailed logging for SSH, administrators can track login attempts, including failed logins, successful logins, and the IP addresses from which the attempts originated. These logs can provide valuable insights into potential attack attempts, such as repeated failed login attempts from a specific IP address or the use of known bad usernames. Regularly reviewing SSH logs can help administrators detect attacks early and take corrective actions before significant damage occurs. Tools like auditd and centralized logging systems like Security Information and Event Management (SIEM) solutions can be used to aggregate and analyze SSH logs, providing a more comprehensive view of server activity and improving response times.

Another key aspect of SSH security is ensuring that the server is configured to limit access to SSH on specific ports. By default, SSH operates on port 22, which is well-known and often targeted by attackers. One of the simplest ways to reduce the risk of automated attacks is to change the default SSH port to a non-standard one. While this is not a foolproof security measure on its own, it can help reduce the volume of automated scanning and probing that targets port 22. Changing the default port can make it more difficult for attackers to find the SSH service, as they would need to perform additional reconnaissance to locate the service. However, administrators should still rely on more robust security measures, such as public key authentication and rate limiting, to effectively secure SSH access.

Network-level security controls are also essential for securing SSH. Administrators should consider configuring firewalls to restrict SSH access to only trusted IP addresses or ranges. This ensures that only specific systems or networks can connect to the SSH service, further reducing the attack surface. Additionally, Virtual Private Networks (VPNs) can be used to ensure that SSH access is only available to authorized users within the corporate network. By requiring users to connect via a VPN before accessing SSH, administrators can further control who can access the server and prevent unauthorized access from outside the trusted network.

Finally, keeping the SSH server and related software up to date is critical to maintaining its security. Vulnerabilities in SSH implementations or related software can be exploited by attackers to gain unauthorized access or execute malicious code. Regularly updating the SSH server software, as well as the underlying operating system and any related packages, ensures that known vulnerabilities are patched and that the server is protected against emerging threats. Automated update mechanisms and regular security audits can help ensure that the server remains secure and that any security patches are applied in a timely manner.

Hardening SSH for secure remote administration is essential for protecting servers from unauthorized access and ensuring the confidentiality of sensitive data. By implementing secure authentication methods, restricting access, enabling logging and monitoring, and applying best practices for configuration, organizations can significantly reduce the risk of attacks. SSH hardening is not a one-time task but an ongoing process that requires vigilance, regular updates, and continuous monitoring to stay ahead of evolving threats. Through these practices, administrators can ensure that remote administration remains secure and that critical systems are protected from malicious activity.

Protecting Against Malware and Ransomware Attacks

Malware and ransomware attacks are among the most dangerous and prevalent cybersecurity threats faced by organizations and individuals alike. These malicious programs can cause significant damage, including data theft, system outages, financial loss, and reputational harm. Malware encompasses a broad range of harmful software, including viruses, worms, spyware, and trojans, while ransomware is a specific type of malware that encrypts files and demands payment for their release. As cybercriminals continue to develop more sophisticated techniques, protecting against malware and ransomware attacks has become a critical aspect of any comprehensive cybersecurity strategy. To effectively defend against these threats, organizations must implement a combination of preventive measures, detection mechanisms, and response strategies.

One of the most important steps in protecting against malware and ransomware is ensuring that all systems and software are regularly updated. Software vendors routinely release patches and security updates to address vulnerabilities that could be exploited by malicious actors. These vulnerabilities are often the target of malware and ransomware attacks. If organizations fail to apply these updates in a timely manner, they leave their systems open to exploitation. Regular patch management is essential to closing security gaps that could be leveraged by cybercriminals. Automated update systems can help ensure that critical updates are applied without delay, but administrators should also monitor for the release of major security patches and apply them as needed. Keeping all systems, from operating systems to applications and third-party software, up to date is a fundamental defense against these types of attacks.

In addition to keeping software updated, it is crucial to implement strong endpoint protection measures. Endpoint protection refers to the security of devices, such as workstations, laptops, and mobile devices, that connect to the network. These endpoints are often the primary entry points for malware and ransomware. Antivirus and anti-malware software should be installed on all endpoints to detect and remove malicious programs before they can cause harm. These tools use signature-based detection methods to identify known threats, as well as heuristic and behavioral analysis to detect new or unknown malware based on suspicious activity patterns. Endpoint protection should also include firewalls to block unauthorized network access and prevent malware from communicating with external command-and-control servers. By securing endpoints, organizations can reduce the risk of malware infections and ransomware attacks that may originate from compromised devices.

Another essential component of defending against malware and ransomware attacks is user education and awareness. Many attacks are successful because users unknowingly execute malicious files or fall victim to phishing scams. Cybercriminals often use social engineering techniques to trick users into opening email attachments, clicking on links, or visiting compromised websites that deliver malware. Training employees on the risks of phishing, the importance of cautious browsing habits, and the dangers of downloading files from untrusted sources is a critical defense mechanism. Organizations should regularly conduct awareness training and simulated phishing campaigns to keep employees vigilant and help them recognize suspicious behavior. Additionally, organizations should encourage the use of strong, unique passwords and implement multi-factor authentication (MFA) to prevent unauthorized access in case of credential theft.

Network segmentation is another powerful strategy for limiting the impact of malware and ransomware attacks. By dividing the network into separate segments or zones, organizations can contain the spread of malware or ransomware within a limited area. For example, critical systems or sensitive data should be isolated from less critical parts of the network. This approach makes it more difficult for malware to propagate across the entire network, as the infection would have to bypass multiple layers of security to spread from one segment to another. In the case of a ransomware attack, network segmentation can prevent the ransomware from encrypting files across all systems, reducing the overall damage. Proper network segmentation can be achieved through the use of virtual LANs (VLANs), firewalls, and access control lists (ACLs) to restrict traffic between segments and limit access to sensitive resources.

Regular data backups are another crucial element of defending against ransomware attacks. Ransomware typically encrypts the victim's files and demands payment for the decryption key. If an organization's data is not backed up properly, it may be forced to pay the ransom to recover its files. However, if data is backed up regularly and stored in a secure location, such as an offline or cloud-based backup, the organization can restore its data without paying the ransom. Backup systems should be tested regularly to ensure that data can be restored quickly and accurately. Backup data should be encrypted to prevent it from being compromised in case of an attack, and backup systems should be isolated from the main network to prevent malware from reaching them. By maintaining regular and secure backups, organizations can minimize the impact of a ransomware attack and avoid the costly consequences of paying a ransom.

In addition to preventive measures, having a robust incident response plan is essential for effectively dealing with malware and ransomware attacks. An incident response plan outlines the steps that should be taken when a cyberattack is detected, helping organizations respond quickly to minimize damage and restore normal operations. The plan should include procedures for isolating infected systems, identifying the source of the attack, containing the spread of malware, and communicating with stakeholders. It should also address how to handle legal and regulatory requirements, such as notifying affected individuals in the case of a data breach. Regularly testing the incident response plan through tabletop exercises or simulated attacks ensures that all team members know their roles and responsibilities during an actual event. A well-practiced incident response plan allows organizations to respond swiftly and efficiently, reducing the downtime and potential damage caused by an attack.

Threat intelligence sharing and collaboration with other organizations can also play a significant role in protecting against malware and ransomware attacks. Cybercriminals frequently target multiple organizations with the same or similar attack methods. By sharing information about emerging threats and attack tactics with other organizations, industry groups, or government agencies, organizations can gain early insights into potential threats and better prepare for attacks. Threat intelligence feeds provide real-time information on known malware signatures, attack patterns, and malicious IP addresses, enabling organizations to update their defenses proactively. Collaborating with trusted partners and staying informed about the latest trends in malware and ransomware attacks helps organizations stay ahead of cybercriminals and strengthen their overall security posture.

Finally, organizations should regularly audit their security systems and perform vulnerability assessments to identify weaknesses that could be exploited by malware or ransomware. Regular security audits help ensure that security controls are functioning as intended and that new vulnerabilities are promptly addressed. Penetration testing, vulnerability scanning, and red teaming can identify potential entry points for malware and ransomware, allowing organizations to fix these weaknesses before they are exploited by attackers. By continuously evaluating and improving their security measures, organizations can reduce the risk of a successful attack and better protect their data and systems.

Protecting against malware and ransomware attacks requires a multi-layered approach that combines preventive measures, user education, network segmentation, data backups, incident response, and continuous monitoring. By implementing these strategies, organizations can significantly reduce the risk of falling victim to cyberattacks and minimize the potential damage caused by these threats. Given the evolving nature of malware and ransomware, organizations must remain vigilant, regularly updating their defenses and staying informed about the latest threats in order to safeguard their systems, data, and reputation.

Securing Virtualization Environments

As organizations continue to embrace virtualization technologies, the need to secure virtual environments becomes more critical. Virtualization offers significant benefits, such as cost savings, improved scalability, and easier management of IT resources. However, it also introduces new security challenges that must be addressed to ensure the integrity, confidentiality, and availability of both virtual machines (VMs) and the underlying infrastructure. Virtualized environments, particularly in data centers and cloud platforms, are prime targets for cybercriminals because of their complexity, multi-tenancy, and high concentration of valuable data and workloads. Securing these environments requires a combination of best practices, tools, and a deep understanding of the unique security risks associated with virtualization.

One of the most fundamental aspects of securing a virtualized environment is to ensure that the hypervisor—the software that enables virtualization—remains secure. The hypervisor plays a critical role in managing and allocating resources to virtual machines, and if compromised, an attacker could gain control over the entire virtualized infrastructure. Hypervisor security should be a top priority when securing a virtualized environment. This includes applying the latest security patches and updates to the hypervisor, as vulnerabilities in hypervisor software can be exploited by attackers to gain unauthorized access to the host system or other virtual machines. In addition, administrators should configure the hypervisor to run with the least amount of privileges necessary to perform its functions, minimizing the potential attack surface. Limiting access to the hypervisor management interfaces and ensuring that these interfaces are secured with strong authentication methods are also critical measures in protecting against unauthorized access.

To further enhance hypervisor security, it is essential to segment and isolate virtual machines from one another. Virtualization environments often host multiple VMs, each with potentially different security requirements. Isolating VMs ensures that even if one virtual machine is compromised, the attacker cannot move laterally to other VMs or access the host system. This isolation can be achieved through the use of virtual networks, firewalls, and access control policies that restrict communication between VMs unless necessary. By implementing strict network segmentation, organizations can prevent attackers from exploiting weaknesses in one VM to gain access to others. Additionally, the use of virtual private networks (VPNs) or other secure communication channels for VM-to-VM communication helps ensure that data transmitted within the virtualized environment remains encrypted and protected from interception.

Another critical aspect of securing virtualization environments is to ensure the security of virtual machines themselves. Each virtual machine should be treated as a separate entity with its own security configuration. The operating system and applications within each VM should be hardened, just as they would be in a physical machine. This includes disabling unnecessary services, installing security patches, and implementing strong user authentication measures. Virtual machines should also be equipped with antivirus and anti-malware software to protect against malicious software that could compromise the VM or spread to other parts of the environment. Administrators should also monitor the activity of VMs for signs of malicious behavior or abnormal resource usage, which could indicate a security breach. Virtual machines should be regularly backed up and stored in secure locations to ensure that they can be recovered in the event of an attack or failure.

Managing the security of virtual machines involves the use of tools such as security information and event management (SIEM) systems, which aggregate and analyze logs from various components of the virtualization environment. These logs can provide valuable insights into the activity of the hypervisor, VMs, and network traffic. By continuously monitoring these logs, administrators can detect suspicious activity, unauthorized access attempts, or abnormal resource utilization patterns that may indicate the presence of malware or an ongoing attack. Automated alerts should be set up to notify administrators of any anomalies, enabling a rapid response to potential security incidents. Moreover, using a centralized logging system ensures that all security events across the virtualized infrastructure can be quickly reviewed, analyzed, and acted upon.

In addition to securing the virtual machines and the hypervisor, network security within virtualized environments must be a key focus. The network infrastructure that connects virtual machines and the underlying host systems can be a vulnerable point if not properly secured. Virtual switches, which manage the communication between VMs and between VMs and external networks, must be configured securely. Access control lists (ACLs) and firewall rules should be used to restrict access to virtual networks, ensuring that only authorized VMs and users can communicate with one another. Network traffic should be monitored for signs of malicious activity, such as port scanning, DDoS attacks, or unauthorized data transfers. Intrusion detection and prevention systems (IDS/IPS) can be deployed within the virtual network to detect and mitigate potential threats in real-time.

Another important element of securing virtualized environments is ensuring the physical security of the underlying infrastructure. Despite the abstract nature of virtualization, the physical servers that host virtual machines are still vulnerable to attacks, whether from malicious insiders or external attackers. Physical access controls, such as locking data center doors, restricting access to authorized personnel, and implementing security cameras, are essential for protecting the hardware that hosts virtual environments. Additionally, the underlying storage infrastructure must be secured to prevent unauthorized access to data stored on physical disks or network-attached storage. Data encryption, both at rest and in transit, is critical to ensure that even if an attacker gains access to the physical infrastructure, they cannot read or manipulate the data stored in virtual machines.

Backup and disaster recovery planning are also crucial aspects of securing virtualized environments. Virtual machines, like physical servers, are vulnerable to data loss due to hardware failure, software corruption, or cyberattacks such as ransomware. Regular backups of virtual machines, along with the underlying configurations and settings, should be performed to ensure that the environment can be restored in the event of a disaster. These backups should be encrypted and stored securely, either in offsite data centers or in the cloud, to protect against physical theft or local disasters. A disaster recovery plan should be in place, detailing the steps required to restore the virtualized environment to full functionality in the event of a system failure or attack. The recovery process should be tested regularly to ensure that the environment can be quickly restored without data loss.

Managing access control and user privileges is another critical component of securing virtualized environments. Access to the hypervisor, virtual machines, and associated resources should be tightly controlled, with only authorized personnel granted administrative rights. Role-based access controls (RBAC) can be used to assign different levels of access to different users, ensuring that only those with the appropriate privileges can modify settings or manage virtual machines. In addition, multi-factor authentication (MFA) should be implemented for accessing sensitive components of the virtualization infrastructure to add an additional layer of security.

As virtualization technology continues to evolve, so do the security risks associated with it. Organizations must stay informed about the latest threats and security practices, continuously adapting their security strategies to meet the demands of the modern virtualized environment. Regular security assessments, vulnerability scanning, and penetration testing should be conducted to identify potential weaknesses and ensure that the environment remains secure against emerging threats. By proactively securing the hypervisor, virtual machines, network, storage, and physical infrastructure, organizations can minimize the risks associated with virtualization and ensure that their virtualized environments remain secure, resilient, and reliable.

Using SELinux and AppArmor for Enhanced Security

In the realm of Linux-based operating systems, security is a top priority. With the growing number of cyber threats targeting both enterprise and personal environments, it is critical to implement robust security measures to safeguard sensitive data, prevent unauthorized access, and protect against potential system breaches. Two of the most effective security modules available for enhancing Linux security are SELinux (Security-Enhanced Linux) and AppArmor. Both of these tools provide mandatory access control (MAC) to complement traditional discretionary access control (DAC), which is typically used in standard Linux systems. By using SELinux and AppArmor, administrators can enforce stricter security policies, limit the damage from compromised applications, and mitigate the risk of system vulnerabilities being exploited.

SELinux is a security module for the Linux kernel that provides a framework for supporting access control policies. Initially developed by the National Security Agency (NSA) in collaboration with Red Hat, SELinux enforces mandatory access control by defining security policies that govern how processes, users, and files interact with one another within the system. SELinux uses a policy-driven approach, which means that administrators define access controls that restrict what a process can do based on security labels attached to files, processes, and other resources. These security labels categorize the various components of the system, and SELinux ensures that each process is only allowed to access files or execute actions according to the policies defined by the system administrator. This allows for fine-grained control over what resources a process can access, reducing the risk of unauthorized access or the spread of an attack within the system.

AppArmor, on the other hand, is another Linux security module that provides mandatory access control, but it differs from SELinux in its approach. While SELinux is more complex and granular, AppArmor focuses on simplicity and ease of use. AppArmor provides a set of predefined profiles for commonly used applications, and administrators can modify these profiles to specify exactly what actions an application is allowed to perform. Rather than using security labels to assign permissions to resources, AppArmor uses path-based security profiles, which restrict an application's access based on the file system paths it needs to interact with. This method provides an intuitive way to secure applications without requiring deep knowledge of security policy management. AppArmor is often considered easier to configure and manage than SELinux, making it a popular choice for administrators who want to enhance security without the complexity of SELinux.

Both SELinux and AppArmor aim to reduce the attack surface by preventing applications from performing unauthorized actions. In a typical Linux system, DAC controls allow users or processes to access resources based on ownership and permission settings. While this model works for many use cases, it can leave gaps in security. For example, if an attacker successfully exploits a vulnerability in an application, they may gain access to resources or perform actions that the application is not supposed to have access to. This is where SELinux and AppArmor come into play. By enforcing policies that restrict processes based on their security labels (SELinux) or file paths (AppArmor), these tools prevent malicious applications from accessing unauthorized resources, even if they have compromised the system.

One of the most significant advantages of SELinux and AppArmor is their ability to enforce least privilege. By ensuring that processes only have the minimum required permissions to perform their tasks, these tools limit the potential damage that can be done by a compromised application. For example, if a web server running on a Linux system is compromised, SELinux or AppArmor would prevent it from accessing sensitive data or executing malicious code. This containment strategy helps to prevent lateral movement within the system and minimizes the impact of an attack. Even if an attacker gains control over an application, the security policies enforced by SELinux or AppArmor prevent them from escalating privileges or accessing sensitive resources.

SELinux, with its comprehensive policy framework, allows for highly granular control over system resources. It provides a wide range of security options, including enforcing access controls based on user roles, file types, and processes. SELinux's flexibility makes it ideal for complex enterprise environments where different processes and users need varying levels of access to different resources. However, this flexibility comes with complexity. Configuring SELinux policies requires a thorough understanding of how SELinux works and how to write or modify policies to fit the needs of the organization. Administrators must also be careful to avoid misconfigurations, as improper policies can inadvertently block legitimate actions or cause system instability.

AppArmor, in contrast, is easier to configure and maintain. Its path-based security model makes it more user-friendly for administrators who may not be well-versed in advanced security policy management. AppArmor uses a profile for each application that defines what files and resources the application is allowed to access and what actions it is permitted to perform. These profiles are typically easier to write and modify compared to the more complex policy files used by SELinux. This simplicity makes AppArmor an attractive choice for organizations that need to secure their systems quickly and with minimal overhead, without requiring deep expertise in security configuration.

While both SELinux and AppArmor are powerful security tools, their choice and implementation depend on the specific needs and requirements of the organization. SELinux is more suitable for environments that require a high level of control over security and can accommodate the complexity of writing and managing security policies. It is commonly used in enterprise-level systems, particularly those running critical applications where security is paramount. On the other hand, AppArmor is more suitable for smaller organizations or those that need to secure specific applications quickly without extensive configuration. AppArmor is often used in environments where ease of use and simplicity are priorities, such as on personal systems or in smaller-scale deployments.

Despite their differences, both SELinux and AppArmor play an essential role in enhancing the security of Linux systems. By providing mandatory access control, they act as a safety net that prevents applications and processes from performing malicious or unintended actions. These tools can be particularly effective when used alongside other security measures, such as firewalls, intrusion detection systems, and antivirus software. Together, these layers of protection create a robust security posture that significantly reduces the risk of a successful attack.

For organizations looking to implement SELinux or AppArmor, there are several best practices to follow. First, both tools should be enabled and configured at the earliest stages of system deployment, rather than added later as an afterthought. It is also essential to regularly review and update security policies and application profiles to ensure they are up-to-date with changing system configurations and emerging threats. Continuous monitoring and logging should be implemented to detect and respond to any potential security incidents or policy violations. Additionally, administrators should ensure that security training is provided to staff to help them understand the tools and how to manage them effectively.

In a world where cyber threats are increasingly sophisticated, using tools like SELinux and AppArmor is essential to securing Linux systems. By enforcing strict access controls and minimizing the attack surface, these tools provide a critical layer of defense against unauthorized access and malicious activities. Whether for large-scale enterprise environments or smaller-scale deployments, SELinux and AppArmor help ensure that Linux systems remain secure, resilient, and protected from evolving threats.

Protecting Against Insider Threats and Privilege Escalation

In the landscape of modern cybersecurity, organizations are increasingly focused on protecting themselves from external threats. While this focus is important, it can sometimes lead to a dangerous oversight: insider threats. An insider threat refers to a security risk that originates from within the organization, typically from an employee, contractor, or business partner who has inside information regarding the organization's systems and operations. Insiders have an inherent advantage over external attackers, as they often have trusted access to networks, systems, and sensitive data. This makes them potentially more dangerous and difficult to detect. Protecting against insider threats and mitigating the risk of privilege escalation are two critical aspects of an organization's overall security posture.

The first step in mitigating insider threats is to limit and manage access to sensitive information. The principle of least privilege should be applied throughout the organization, ensuring that individuals only have access to the data and systems necessary for their roles. By doing so, the impact of a compromised account or insider attack is limited, as unauthorized individuals are restricted from accessing critical systems or sensitive data. For example, an employee in the finance department should only have access to financial data and systems, not to proprietary source code or sensitive HR records. This minimizes the amount of potentially valuable information that any one person can steal, misuse, or otherwise exploit. Implementing access controls, including robust authentication mechanisms and role-based access control (RBAC), ensures that employees are only granted the minimum level of access required for their job functions.

Additionally, monitoring user activity is essential for detecting and preventing insider threats. When individuals have access to sensitive systems, their actions should be logged and regularly reviewed. Monitoring systems can track login attempts, file access, data modifications, and other suspicious activities. By reviewing these logs, administrators can identify anomalies or unusual patterns of behavior that may indicate malicious intent. For instance, if an employee accesses data outside of their typical working hours or tries to access resources they do not typically use, it could be an indication of a security breach or an attempt to gather sensitive information for malicious purposes. Effective monitoring requires automated systems that can alert security teams to suspicious activities in real time, enabling them to respond quickly to mitigate potential risks.

Insider threats are not always malicious. Sometimes, the threat comes from careless or negligent behavior. Employees who are not well-trained in security best practices may inadvertently cause security breaches, such as by using weak passwords, falling for phishing scams, or sharing confidential information with unauthorized individuals. This is why employee education and awareness are critical components of any insider threat mitigation strategy. Regular training sessions can educate staff about common security risks, such as social engineering attacks, phishing, and the importance of using strong passwords. Additionally, promoting a culture of security awareness, where security is considered a shared responsibility, helps ensure that employees take the necessary precautions to protect sensitive data and systems.

When it comes to preventing privilege escalation, it is important to have a system in place that ensures users' permissions are carefully monitored and controlled. Privilege escalation occurs when an individual gains elevated access to resources or systems that they are not authorized to use, typically by exploiting a vulnerability or misconfiguration. Attackers, whether external or internal, may attempt to escalate their privileges in order to gain control over critical systems or to access sensitive data. Preventing privilege escalation begins with secure system configuration and the principle of least privilege. For example, administrators should avoid giving users more privileges than necessary, such as granting unnecessary administrative access or the ability to install software. Additionally, systems should be configured to restrict the execution of privileged commands or applications to only authorized users.

One important strategy for protecting against privilege escalation is the use of multi-factor authentication (MFA). MFA requires users to provide two or more verification factors, such as a password and a fingerprint scan, before gaining access to sensitive systems or performing privileged actions. This makes it significantly more difficult for an attacker to escalate privileges, as they would need to compromise multiple authentication factors rather than just obtaining a user's password. MFA can be applied to high-risk areas of the organization, such as administrative accounts or systems that store sensitive data, ensuring that only authorized users can perform actions that could lead to privilege escalation.

Additionally, organizations should regularly audit user accounts and permissions to ensure that they align with the principle of least privilege. As employees move between roles, change responsibilities, or leave the company, their access rights should be updated accordingly. Former employees should have their accounts and access rights immediately revoked to prevent them from retaining access to sensitive systems after their departure. Regular audits of user accounts can help identify any over-privileged accounts or accounts that no longer need access to certain systems. Automation tools can assist in auditing permissions across multiple systems and provide reports that highlight discrepancies, making it easier for administrators to rectify issues before they are exploited.

Another essential element in preventing privilege escalation is the implementation of strong segmentation within the network. By creating network zones with different levels of access, administrators can control how users and systems interact with one another. For example, sensitive data or critical systems should be isolated from general users or less secure parts of the network. This segmentation ensures that even if a user's account is compromised, the attacker will be limited in their ability to access other parts of the network or escalate their privileges to more sensitive areas. Intrusion detection and prevention systems (IDPS) can also be employed to monitor for suspicious activity that may indicate an attempted privilege escalation. These systems can alert administrators if abnormal access patterns or unauthorized commands are detected, providing an additional layer of defense against privilege escalation attempts.

One of the most effective ways to protect against both insider threats and privilege escalation is the use of endpoint detection and response (EDR) solutions. EDR systems continuously monitor and collect data from endpoint devices such as computers, mobile devices, and servers. They can detect suspicious behaviors, such as the use of unauthorized tools or attempts to bypass security controls, and automatically respond by blocking the malicious activity or alerting security teams. By deploying EDR across all endpoints in the organization, administrators can quickly detect and respond to attempts at privilege escalation, as well as identify any potential insider threats before they can cause significant damage.

In addition to implementing technical measures, creating a comprehensive incident response plan is vital for addressing insider threats and privilege escalation incidents when they occur. The plan should outline the steps to take if an insider is suspected of malicious behavior or if privilege escalation is detected. Having a predefined response procedure helps minimize confusion and ensures that appropriate actions are taken promptly. It is also important to have clear communication channels in place for reporting suspicious activities, and the organization should maintain an effective system for investigating and addressing security incidents.

In an age where data is an organization's most valuable asset, protecting against insider threats and privilege escalation is essential for maintaining trust, security, and operational continuity. By implementing a combination of strong access controls, employee training, monitoring systems, and incident response procedures, organizations can effectively safeguard themselves from these internal threats. These strategies create a layered defense that minimizes the risk of unauthorized access, reduces the potential damage from insider threats, and ensures that systems remain secure even in the face of attempts to escalate privileges.

Role-Based Access Control (RBAC) for Servers

Role-Based Access Control (RBAC) is a security model used to regulate access to computer systems, applications, and networks based on the roles of individual users within an organization. In RBAC, each user is assigned one or more roles, and each role has specific permissions associated with it. This method helps organizations implement the principle of least privilege, ensuring that users have only the minimum level of access necessary to perform their job functions. For servers, where data and resources are often sensitive and critical to business operations, RBAC is an essential framework for managing access control efficiently and securely.

The primary purpose of RBAC is to streamline the management of user permissions and reduce the risk of unauthorized access. In traditional access control models, managing permissions for each individual user can be a complex and error-prone process. However, with RBAC, users are grouped into roles, and permissions are granted to roles rather than individual users. This simplifies the management of permissions because when a user changes roles or is added to a role, their permissions are automatically adjusted based on the role's associated access rights. For example, an administrator might assign different roles such as "admin," "developer," or "support," each with different access levels to the server. The admin role might have full control over the server, while the developer role may have access only to specific applications or directories, and the support role may only have read access to certain logs or monitoring tools.

RBAC helps to enforce the principle of least privilege by ensuring that users only have access to resources that are necessary for their role. For instance, a server administrator needs access to system configurations and management tools but should not have access to the sensitive data stored on the server unless explicitly required. Similarly, a user working in a specific department may need access only to the data related to their department and should not be able to access confidential information from other departments. By assigning users to predefined roles and limiting access to necessary resources, organizations can significantly reduce the risk of insider threats and accidental data leaks. With this model, the risk of privilege escalation is minimized, as users are not granted excessive permissions that could potentially be exploited by attackers.

One of the most important aspects of RBAC for servers is its ability to support hierarchical roles. In a hierarchical RBAC system, roles can inherit permissions from other roles, allowing for a more flexible and scalable way to manage user access. For example, in a server environment, there might be a "read-only" role that allows users to view system logs but not modify them. A higher-level role, such as "operator," might inherit the read-only permissions but also be granted the ability to restart services. This hierarchical structure enables administrators to define clear and logical relationships between roles and simplifies the process of managing user permissions as the organization grows. When new roles are needed or existing roles require changes, administrators can modify the parent roles, and these changes will automatically cascade to all child roles, ensuring consistency across the system.

RBAC also simplifies compliance with regulatory requirements. Many industries have strict data protection laws and regulations that dictate who can access certain types of information. For example, healthcare organizations are required to comply with the Health Insurance Portability and Accountability Act (HIPAA), which mandates that only authorized individuals have access to patient data. Similarly, financial institutions must comply with regulations like the Payment Card Industry Data Security Standard (PCI DSS), which defines strict access controls over payment card information. By using RBAC, organizations can implement access control policies that are in line with these regulations, ensuring that users have appropriate access to sensitive data and that this access is auditable. Role-based access can also help with data segmentation, making it easier to implement and enforce access restrictions across different servers and applications, which is critical for compliance.

In practice, RBAC on servers is typically implemented using operating system features or third-party access control systems. For example, on Linux servers, RBAC can be enforced using tools such as SELinux (Security-Enhanced Linux) or AppArmor, which integrate with the Linux kernel to control access based on user roles and security policies. These tools allow administrators to define fine-grained access controls, specifying which users or roles can execute particular commands, read specific files, or modify system settings. On Windows servers, RBAC can be implemented using Active Directory (AD), which manages user roles and permissions centrally across the network. Active Directory allows administrators to define roles such as "administrator," "user," and "guest," with each role having different levels of access to the server and its resources.

Effective RBAC implementation also involves maintaining and regularly reviewing role definitions and user access. Over time, organizations evolve, and employees change roles, move to different departments, or leave the company. It is essential to have processes in place to ensure that user access is reviewed regularly to ensure that permissions remain aligned with users' job responsibilities. This can be achieved through regular audits and reviews of user accounts and roles. When employees change roles, administrators should adjust their permissions to reflect their new responsibilities and ensure that they no longer have access to resources that are not relevant to their new role. Similarly, when employees leave the company, administrators should promptly revoke their access to all systems, including servers, to prevent unauthorized access from former employees. Implementing a periodic review of user roles helps to maintain a secure environment and prevents the accumulation of unnecessary privileges.

RBAC also provides a clear audit trail that can be valuable for identifying and responding to security incidents. Because user actions are associated with specific roles and permissions, administrators can track what users have done and identify who was responsible for a particular action. For example, if an incident occurs, such as unauthorized access to sensitive data, administrators can trace the actions back to the role associated with the user who initiated the access. This helps with identifying the root cause of security incidents and can be useful for compliance reporting, where organizations need to demonstrate that they are following appropriate access control procedures.

While RBAC is a powerful tool for securing servers and managing user access, it is important to ensure that it is implemented alongside other security measures. For instance, combining RBAC with multi-factor authentication (MFA) can provide an additional layer of security, ensuring that even if a user's credentials are compromised, unauthorized access is still prevented. In addition, network segmentation and firewalls can help further restrict access to servers and resources, making it harder for unauthorized users to access sensitive areas of the network. Monitoring and logging user activity across servers can also help detect suspicious behavior, alerting administrators to potential breaches before they escalate.

RBAC for servers is an essential tool for managing user access, protecting sensitive data, and reducing the risk of security breaches. By assigning permissions based on roles and ensuring that users only have access to the resources necessary for their job functions, organizations can effectively implement the principle of least privilege. Role-based access control not only simplifies the management of permissions but also enhances security, compliance, and auditing processes. As the organization grows and evolves, RBAC ensures that user access remains consistent, secure, and aligned with business needs, providing a robust foundation for server security and risk management.

Hardening Network Configuration and Routing

In the world of network security, one of the most critical areas of focus is the configuration and management of network devices, such as routers, switches, and firewalls, which form the backbone of any organization's communication infrastructure. Properly securing network configurations and routing protocols is vital to ensure the confidentiality, integrity, and availability of data as it flows across the network. By implementing hardened network configurations and secure routing practices, organizations can mitigate the risk of unauthorized access, attacks, and network disruptions. This chapter discusses the key practices and considerations for hardening network configuration and routing to improve overall network security.

The first step in securing a network is configuring network devices with a minimal set of services and features that are necessary for the organization's operations. Many network devices, such as routers and switches, come with a wide array of default settings and services that may not be needed. These excess services present potential attack vectors that could be exploited by attackers. For example, remote management services such as Telnet or HTTP may be enabled by default, but they often send data in an unencrypted form, making them vulnerable to interception. Disabling unnecessary services and ensuring that only essential features are enabled reduces the potential attack surface of the network devices. Additionally, default configurations, which are often well-known to attackers, should be changed. Default passwords, login names, and SNMP community strings must be updated to strong, unique credentials to prevent unauthorized access.

Access control is another essential element of hardening network configurations. Network devices should be configured to restrict access to only authorized personnel and trusted devices. One common method is to implement Access Control Lists (ACLs), which define which users or devices are allowed to communicate with specific network resources. ACLs can be used to filter traffic and prevent unauthorized access to sensitive parts of the network. For instance, a router might be configured with an ACL that only allows traffic from specific IP addresses or ranges to access certain internal resources. Similarly, network devices should be segmented into different zones with distinct security policies, ensuring that different areas of the network have the appropriate level of access control.

In addition to ACLs, strong authentication mechanisms should be implemented for network devices. A password policy that requires complex, multi-character passwords should be enforced, and devices should use more secure methods of authentication, such as SSH for remote access instead of less secure protocols like Telnet. Multi-factor authentication (MFA) can be applied to increase security further. With MFA, even if an attacker is able to obtain login credentials, they would still need access to a second authentication factor, such as a token or biometric scan, to gain access. This adds an additional layer of security and makes it more difficult for unauthorized users to access critical network devices.

Network segmentation is another powerful security measure that should be used to improve network configuration. By segmenting the network into multiple subnets or VLANs, an organization can restrict the flow of traffic between different parts of the network. This is particularly useful for isolating critical systems or sensitive data from the rest of the network. For example, servers that handle financial transactions or personally identifiable information (PII) could be placed on a separate subnet with restricted access from other areas of the network. This limits the impact of any potential breach, as an attacker who gains access to one part of the network will not easily be able to move laterally across the entire infrastructure. Network segmentation also improves performance by reducing unnecessary traffic between segments and optimizing network resources.

Another important aspect of network hardening is securing routing protocols, which are responsible for determining how data is forwarded across networks. Routing protocols, such as Open Shortest Path First (OSPF) and Border Gateway Protocol (BGP), are crucial for enabling communication between different networks. However, these protocols can also be vulnerable to attacks, such as route hijacking or man-in-the-middle attacks, if not properly secured. One key measure is to implement route filtering, which ensures that only valid routing information is exchanged between routers. This can prevent attackers from injecting malicious routing updates that could cause traffic to be rerouted to unauthorized destinations. Additionally, routers should be configured to use authentication for routing protocol exchanges to ensure that only trusted routers are allowed to exchange routing information. For example, OSPF and BGP support authentication mechanisms that use passwords or digital certificates to validate routing updates, helping to prevent unauthorized devices from influencing the network's routing decisions.

Encryption plays a vital role in securing network traffic, especially when data is transmitted over untrusted or public networks. One common method for encrypting traffic is the use of Virtual Private Networks (VPNs), which create secure tunnels for data transmission between devices across the internet. When configuring network devices, administrators should ensure that VPNs are properly configured to use strong encryption protocols, such as IPsec or SSL, to protect sensitive data. VPNs not only encrypt traffic but also provide authentication to ensure that only authorized users can access the network. Secure connections should be enforced for management interfaces, ensuring that all remote administrative access to network devices is encrypted to prevent data interception or tampering.

Monitoring network traffic is also a critical part of securing network configurations. Continuous monitoring helps administrators identify unusual patterns, unauthorized access attempts, or signs of a potential attack. Intrusion detection and prevention systems (IDPS) can be deployed to monitor network traffic in real-time and alert administrators to suspicious activities. For example, if an attacker tries to scan network devices or launch a DoS attack, the IDPS can detect the anomaly and take appropriate action, such as blocking the malicious IP or alerting security teams. Regular traffic analysis and log review can also help identify misconfigurations, performance issues, or potential vulnerabilities that could be exploited by attackers.

One of the key elements of hardening network configurations is implementing a robust backup and disaster recovery plan for network settings. Configuration files for network devices, including routers, firewalls, and switches, should be regularly backed up and stored securely. If a configuration is lost or corrupted due to a system failure or attack, it can be restored quickly from the backup, minimizing downtime and ensuring continuity of operations. The backup should also be encrypted and stored in a secure location to prevent unauthorized access.

In addition to configuration hardening, securing physical access to network devices is another important aspect of overall network security. Network devices should be housed in secure locations, such as locked server rooms or data centers, to prevent unauthorized personnel from tampering with or accessing the hardware. Physical security measures, such as surveillance cameras, access control systems, and alarm systems, should be implemented to monitor and control physical access to critical network infrastructure.

Finally, regular audits and reviews of network configurations are essential to maintaining a secure environment. Over time, network configurations may evolve, and new vulnerabilities or threats may emerge. Regular audits allow administrators to assess the effectiveness of existing security measures, identify areas for improvement, and ensure that security patches are applied promptly. Vulnerability scanning and penetration testing can also be performed to detect weaknesses in the network configuration that may have been overlooked.

Hardening network configuration and routing is a fundamental aspect of securing modern IT infrastructures. By implementing strict access controls, securing routing protocols, encrypting network traffic, and regularly monitoring and reviewing configurations, organizations can reduce the risk of attacks and ensure the integrity of their networks. A well-secured network not only protects sensitive data but also enhances the reliability and performance of the entire IT environment, supporting business continuity and safeguarding against potential threats.

Preventing Server Misconfigurations

Server misconfigurations are one of the most common causes of security vulnerabilities in an organization's IT infrastructure. They can expose critical systems to external and internal threats, providing attackers with easy entry points to exploit weaknesses in the system. Server misconfigurations can occur at any stage of the system's lifecycle, from initial deployment to routine updates, and they often arise from human error, lack of proper training, or insufficient security practices. Preventing these misconfigurations is a crucial aspect of securing a server environment, as a single misstep can lead to severe consequences, including unauthorized access, data breaches, and service disruptions. To prevent server misconfigurations, organizations must implement proactive measures that focus on standardization, regular audits, automation, and continuous monitoring.

The first step in preventing server misconfigurations is to establish clear configuration management standards. Standardization ensures that servers across the organization are configured in a consistent and secure manner. This approach reduces the risk of overlooking security best practices or leaving configuration gaps that could be exploited by attackers. Configuration management tools such as Ansible, Chef, or Puppet can be used to automate the configuration of servers, ensuring that all systems are set up according to the organization's security policies and industry best practices. These tools allow administrators to define and enforce standardized configurations, eliminating the variability introduced by manual configuration changes. Automated configuration management also ensures that changes are tracked and documented, providing an audit trail that can help identify misconfigurations when they occur.

Proper server hardening is an essential part of preventing misconfigurations. Hardening refers to the process of reducing the attack surface of a server by disabling unnecessary services, closing unused ports, and applying security patches. During the server setup phase, unnecessary services and software should be removed or disabled. For example, many servers come with default configurations that enable a variety of services that may not be needed, such as Telnet, FTP, or certain administrative interfaces. These services can introduce vulnerabilities if not properly secured. Ensuring that only the services necessary for the server's role are enabled reduces the number of potential attack vectors and simplifies the task of securing the system. Regular hardening practices, including the disabling of unnecessary software and services, should be applied consistently across the server environment.

It is equally important to regularly review and update configurations to ensure they remain secure. Server configurations can quickly become outdated as new vulnerabilities are discovered, or as software and hardware updates are released. Regularly patching servers and updating configuration settings ensures that the server environment remains secure and that known vulnerabilities are addressed promptly. This also involves monitoring for changes that could introduce vulnerabilities, such as updates to security patches or modifications to default configurations. Configurations should be reviewed periodically as part of a routine security audit process, ensuring that all settings align with organizational security policies and industry standards.

Another critical component in preventing server misconfigurations is access control. Ensuring that only authorized individuals have access to configure or modify server settings is essential to maintaining system security. Role-based access control (RBAC) should be implemented to assign permissions based on the user's role within the organization. For example, system administrators may have full access to server configurations, while general users may only be permitted to access specific applications or services. By enforcing strict access control policies, the risk of misconfigurations due to human error or unauthorized access is significantly reduced. Additionally, access to sensitive configuration files should be limited to trusted personnel, and these files should be regularly audited for changes.

Logging and monitoring play a key role in preventing and detecting server misconfigurations. Comprehensive logging allows administrators to track who made changes to a server's configuration, when the changes were made, and what specific modifications were applied. By maintaining detailed logs of server activity, organizations can quickly identify if and when a misconfiguration occurs, allowing them to take corrective action before the issue escalates into a security breach. Automated monitoring tools can also be deployed to track system health and configuration integrity. These tools can alert administrators to potential misconfigurations, such as open ports, weak passwords, or failed security patches, in real time, enabling a prompt response to address the issue.

An important practice in preventing server misconfigurations is the use of security baselines. Security baselines are predefined sets of configurations that follow security best practices for hardening servers. These baselines ensure that all servers are set up with a consistent, secure configuration from the outset. By adhering to established baselines, organizations can reduce the risk of misconfigurations that arise from inconsistent setup practices. Baselines can be based on industry standards, such as the Center for Internet Security (CIS) benchmarks, which provide a comprehensive set of security configurations for various server types and operating systems. Regularly comparing server configurations to the baseline helps identify deviations from security standards, enabling administrators to rectify misconfigurations before they become a security issue.

Automation can greatly reduce the risk of misconfigurations by eliminating the potential for human error. Automated deployment and configuration management tools can ensure that server configurations are consistently applied across all systems. When servers are deployed, configuration settings can be automatically enforced to meet security requirements. This is especially important in large-scale environments, where manual configuration of multiple servers can lead to inconsistencies and overlooked vulnerabilities. Automation also ensures that server configurations are updated in real time, making it easier to maintain a secure environment as the system evolves. Additionally, automated systems allow for faster response times to new security threats, as configuration changes can be applied immediately to all affected servers.

Configuration management tools can also be used in conjunction with vulnerability scanners to identify misconfigurations or weaknesses within the server environment. These scanners analyze server configurations against known security best practices and alert administrators to any deviations from the recommended settings. By integrating vulnerability scanners with configuration management tools, organizations can proactively detect and correct potential misconfigurations before they are exploited by attackers.

Another important aspect of preventing server misconfigurations is educating system administrators and staff about security best practices. Misconfigurations often occur due to a lack of awareness or understanding of secure configuration practices. Training administrators on proper configuration management, the importance of server hardening, and the risks associated with improper configurations can help reduce the likelihood of misconfigurations. Regular training and awareness programs should be implemented to keep staff up to date with the latest security threats and best practices. Additionally, system administrators should be encouraged to follow a standardized process when configuring or updating servers to ensure that all necessary security measures are taken into account.

Lastly, disaster recovery and backup procedures are essential in mitigating the impact of misconfigurations. While prevention is the key focus, it is inevitable that some misconfigurations will slip through. Having a reliable backup and recovery plan in place ensures that if a misconfiguration results in a system failure or breach, the server environment can be restored to a secure state. Backups should be taken regularly and stored securely, and recovery processes should be tested to ensure they are effective and efficient. This allows organizations to quickly restore services and minimize downtime caused by misconfigurations or other security incidents.

Preventing server misconfigurations is a critical aspect of maintaining a secure IT environment. By implementing strong configuration management standards, regularly auditing and updating server settings, and using automation and monitoring tools, organizations can significantly reduce the risk of misconfigurations. Additionally, adhering to security baselines, educating staff, and maintaining robust disaster recovery plans further enhances the ability to prevent and mitigate the impact of misconfigurations. Through these proactive measures, organizations can ensure their servers are securely configured, reducing vulnerabilities and minimizing the potential for security breaches.

The Role of Security Audits in System Hardening

Security audits are a fundamental aspect of any comprehensive cybersecurity strategy, playing a crucial role in the ongoing process of system hardening. These audits are systematic evaluations of a system's security posture, designed to identify vulnerabilities, assess the effectiveness of current security controls, and ensure compliance with security policies and industry standards. Hardening a system involves configuring its security settings to reduce potential risks, and security audits act as a critical mechanism for assessing whether the hardening measures are adequately implemented. By regularly conducting security audits, organizations can not only verify that their systems are secure but also identify areas for improvement, ensuring that their systems remain resilient against evolving threats.

A security audit typically begins with a thorough examination of the organization's infrastructure, including servers, networks, applications, and databases. During this process, auditors assess various aspects of the system, such as user access controls, firewall configurations, encryption settings, and software patch levels. The primary goal is to identify any weaknesses or gaps in the system's defenses that could potentially be exploited by attackers. This includes detecting misconfigurations, outdated software, and improper access controls, which are often overlooked in day-to-day operations but can significantly increase the risk of a security breach. Audits help ensure that all aspects of the system are hardened according to best practices, such as reducing unnecessary services, securing network ports, and enforcing strong authentication methods.

One of the key roles of a security audit is to ensure that the system's security measures are aligned with industry standards and regulatory requirements. Many organizations are required to comply with specific regulations, such as the General Data Protection Regulation (GDPR), the Health Insurance Portability and Accountability Act (HIPAA), or the Payment Card Industry Data Security Standard (PCI DSS). These regulations mandate certain security controls and practices to protect sensitive data and ensure that organizations maintain a strong security posture. A security audit assesses whether the organization's systems comply with these standards and identifies any gaps that need to be addressed. This is particularly important for industries dealing with sensitive customer data or financial transactions, where non-compliance can lead to severe legal consequences and reputational damage.

Moreover, security audits are invaluable for identifying potential insider threats. While external attacks often dominate the conversation around cybersecurity, insider threats, which include malicious actions or unintentional mistakes by employees, contractors, or trusted partners, represent a significant risk. Security audits help detect unusual user activity, such as unauthorized access to sensitive data, privilege escalation attempts, or irregular network traffic patterns. By reviewing system logs, user behavior, and access control policies, auditors can identify signs of internal misuse or negligence and recommend corrective actions to mitigate these risks. Regular audits are an essential tool for maintaining visibility into the actions of users and ensuring that access controls are strictly enforced, reducing the chances of an insider threat compromising the system.

In addition to identifying vulnerabilities and ensuring compliance, security audits provide a valuable opportunity for organizations to evaluate the effectiveness of their existing security policies and controls. As cyber threats evolve, security measures that were once sufficient may no longer be adequate. Audits enable organizations to assess whether their current defenses are capable of protecting against emerging threats. This includes evaluating the performance of intrusion detection and prevention systems, firewalls, antivirus software, and other security tools. Auditors may also examine incident response plans, ensuring that the organization is prepared to respond quickly and effectively in the event of a breach. By continuously assessing and updating security measures based on audit findings, organizations can stay ahead of potential threats and ensure that their defenses remain strong.

Another critical aspect of security audits is the assessment of patch management practices. Many security breaches are the result of unpatched vulnerabilities in software or hardware. Vulnerability management is an ongoing process, and security patches must be applied promptly to address newly discovered threats. Auditors examine the organization's patch management procedures, ensuring that systems are regularly updated with the latest security patches and that any critical vulnerabilities are addressed in a timely manner. They also assess whether patching processes are being followed consistently across all systems, including third-party applications and hardware devices. Inconsistent patch management can leave systems exposed to known threats, and audits help identify areas where patching may be delayed or neglected.

Security audits also play a crucial role in risk management. By identifying vulnerabilities and assessing the likelihood and potential impact of an exploit, audits help organizations prioritize their security efforts. Not all vulnerabilities carry the same level of risk, and audits help determine which weaknesses should be addressed first. For example, an audit might reveal that a system is running outdated software with known vulnerabilities, but the likelihood of an attack exploiting this vulnerability is low due to the lack of external access. On the other hand, an audit may identify an open port on a publicly accessible server that could be used for an attack. Understanding the risks associated with each vulnerability allows organizations to allocate resources more effectively and address the most pressing security concerns first.

Regular security audits also foster a culture of security awareness within the organization. By involving all levels of the organization in the audit process, from system administrators to executives, audits highlight the importance of security in daily operations and decision-making. Audits provide an opportunity for teams to collaborate and address security challenges together, helping to build a more security-conscious organizational culture. Additionally, audits provide valuable feedback that can be used to improve security training and awareness programs. For example, an audit might reveal that employees are not following proper security protocols when accessing sensitive data or using company devices. This feedback can then be used to strengthen training initiatives and reduce human errors that contribute to security vulnerabilities.

The process of conducting security audits can also improve the incident response capabilities of an organization. When an organization experiences a security incident, it is essential to understand how the breach occurred, what systems were affected, and how to prevent similar incidents in the future. Audits help organizations develop incident response procedures that can be activated quickly in the event of a breach. By reviewing audit findings, security teams can identify common attack vectors, analyze past incidents, and refine response strategies to ensure that they can react effectively and minimize the impact of future incidents. This proactive approach to incident response can significantly reduce downtime, data loss, and reputational damage during a security event.

Lastly, security audits should not be viewed as a one-time or periodic task but as part of an ongoing, continuous security improvement process. As new threats emerge, system configurations change, and the organization grows, regular audits ensure that the security posture remains strong and that any new risks are identified and mitigated. By adopting a culture of continuous improvement and regularly performing security audits, organizations can create a resilient security infrastructure capable of responding to evolving threats. Audits are not just a tool for identifying weaknesses but also an opportunity to strengthen and adapt security measures to meet the changing landscape of cybersecurity challenges.

Through regular and thorough security audits, organizations can better safeguard their systems, ensure compliance, and improve their ability to detect and respond to security incidents. The insights gained from these audits enable organizations to make informed decisions, prioritize resources, and implement effective measures to protect their systems from a wide range of threats. With the ever-growing complexity of cyber threats, security audits remain an indispensable element of system hardening and overall cybersecurity strategy.

Protecting Server Hardware Against Physical Threats

When securing an organization's infrastructure, the focus often centers on software, network defenses, and cybersecurity protocols. However, physical security of server hardware is just as critical, if not more so, in ensuring that sensitive data and systems remain protected. Physical threats to server hardware can come in many forms, ranging from natural disasters, such as floods or fires, to human threats like theft, sabotage, or unauthorized access. Without proper physical security measures in place, even the most robust cybersecurity strategies can be undermined by a lack of protection for the hardware that stores and processes valuable information. Protecting server hardware from physical threats is an essential part of any comprehensive security strategy, and it requires a combination of preventive measures, access controls, monitoring, and disaster recovery planning to minimize risks and ensure business continuity.

The first step in protecting server hardware is ensuring that it is housed in a secure, controlled physical environment. Data centers, where servers are typically located, should be protected from unauthorized access by both physical barriers and security personnel. Physical barriers include secure doors, locks, and fences, while additional security features may involve biometric scanners or proximity cards to ensure that only authorized individuals can enter the facility. Proper access control protocols are essential, and staff should undergo background checks to ensure their trustworthiness. Only essential personnel should have access to the server area, and this access should be strictly monitored. Access logs can be used to track who enters and exits the facility, and any suspicious activity should be flagged immediately. By controlling who has physical access to servers, organizations can prevent unauthorized tampering, theft, or sabotage of critical hardware.

To further mitigate the risk of unauthorized access, server rooms and data centers should be monitored using security cameras. Video surveillance allows for the continuous monitoring of the facility and provides a record of any incidents that may occur. Cameras should be strategically placed to cover all entry points, as well as areas where sensitive equipment is stored or operated. In addition to cameras, alarm systems can be installed to alert security personnel to unauthorized attempts to enter the facility, providing an immediate response in case of a breach. This combination of physical barriers, surveillance, and alarm systems helps create a layered defense against potential threats to server hardware.

Environmental threats, such as fires, floods, and extreme temperatures, are another significant concern for server hardware. Servers are sensitive to environmental conditions, and extreme heat or water damage can quickly render them inoperable. To protect against fire, data centers should be equipped with smoke detectors and automatic fire suppression systems. These systems should be carefully selected to ensure they do not harm the equipment, with alternatives such as clean agent fire suppression systems being ideal in server rooms. Flood protection measures should also be in place, including raised flooring to prevent water from reaching equipment and the installation of flood barriers around the facility. Data centers located in flood-prone areas should consider additional precautions, such as flood alarms and drainage systems, to manage excess water. Temperature regulation is another critical factor in the protection of server hardware. Servers generate significant heat during operation, and without proper cooling, they can overheat and malfunction. Adequate ventilation, air conditioning, and redundant cooling systems should be installed to maintain an optimal temperature range and prevent overheating.

In addition to environmental controls, organizations must implement redundancy measures to ensure that their server hardware can withstand unexpected disruptions. This includes the use of uninterruptible power supplies (UPS) to protect against power outages. A UPS system provides backup power to servers in the event of an electrical failure, allowing them to continue operating long enough to either switch to a secondary power source or safely shut down. Redundant power sources, such as backup generators, should also be in place to ensure that power is available even during extended outages. Additionally, redundancy should be applied to the server hardware itself. This includes using multiple hard drives in a RAID (Redundant Array of Independent Disks) configuration, which can protect against data loss in the event of a hardware failure. By ensuring that critical systems have redundant power supplies, cooling systems, and storage solutions, organizations can reduce the risk of prolonged downtime and data loss due to hardware failures or other physical threats.

Physical security for server hardware must also extend to disaster recovery planning. In the event of a catastrophic failure, such as a fire, flood, or theft, organizations need to be able to recover quickly and restore their systems to normal operations. A disaster recovery plan should include regular backups of critical data and configurations, stored securely both on-site and off-site. Off-site backups, such as those stored in a geographically distant data center or in the cloud, protect against local disasters and ensure that data can be recovered even if the primary server facility is destroyed. Recovery processes should be regularly tested to ensure that they are effective and that the organization can quickly recover from any physical disruption to its hardware. Documentation for recovery procedures, along with clear roles and responsibilities for personnel, ensures that the response to a disaster is coordinated and efficient.

In some cases, physical theft of server hardware can pose a significant risk. Servers often contain sensitive data, and if an attacker can physically steal a server or its components, they could gain unauthorized access to this information. To prevent theft, servers should be securely mounted in locked racks or cabinets within the data center. Racks should be equipped with tamper-resistant locks, and cables should be secured to prevent the removal of devices. In addition to securing individual components, physical security measures around the entire facility, such as fencing, secure gates, and guarded entry points, can deter theft. In the case of smaller, less secure server locations, servers should be secured with cable locks or stored in locked, enclosed spaces.

Finally, organizations must maintain proper inventory and asset management practices to ensure that all server hardware is accounted for and secure. This includes tracking hardware locations, serial numbers, and configurations to maintain a comprehensive record of all devices in use. Asset management software can help track the lifecycle of server hardware from procurement to decommissioning, ensuring that devices are properly secured at all times. When hardware is decommissioned, it should be wiped of all sensitive data before disposal, preventing any potential data recovery from discarded equipment. By maintaining strict inventory controls, organizations can reduce the risk of losing track of sensitive hardware and ensure that all assets are properly protected.

Protecting server hardware from physical threats is an often-overlooked aspect of an organization's overall security posture, but it is just as critical as securing software and networks. By implementing comprehensive physical security measures, organizations can significantly reduce the risk of hardware theft, environmental damage, and unauthorized access. A secure server environment relies on a combination of physical access controls, environmental safeguards, redundancy measures, and disaster recovery plans, all of which work together to ensure the integrity and availability of the system. Through these practices, organizations can ensure that their server hardware remains protected, resilient, and capable of supporting the security of their overall IT infrastructure.

Implementing Multi-Factor Authentication for Server Access

As organizations continue to digitize their operations and store critical data on servers, securing access to these systems becomes more vital than ever. Cyberattacks targeting unauthorized access are on the rise, with attackers often exploiting weak or stolen credentials to gain entry into sensitive systems. In this context, relying solely on traditional username and password-based authentication is no longer sufficient to protect against modern threats. Multi-factor authentication (MFA) is a powerful security measure that adds an additional layer of defense to server access by requiring users to provide two or more verification factors to authenticate themselves. Implementing MFA for server access not only strengthens security but also helps mitigate the risks associated with compromised credentials, providing an essential safeguard in today's increasingly complex cybersecurity landscape.

Multi-factor authentication works by combining something the user knows, such as a password, with something the user has, such as a security token, smartphone, or biometric data, or something the user is, such as a fingerprint or retina scan. The goal of MFA is to make it significantly harder for an attacker to gain unauthorized access, even if they have obtained one factor, such as the user's password. For example, if a password is compromised through a phishing attack or a data breach, MFA ensures that the attacker still cannot access the server without the second factor, such as a one-time passcode (OTP) sent to the user's mobile device. This added layer of protection is particularly important for securing servers, where sensitive data, critical applications, and administrative functions are housed.

The first step in implementing MFA for server access is selecting the appropriate authentication factors that align with the organization's security needs and operational environment. Commonly used factors include something the user knows, such as a password or PIN, something the user has, such as a hardware token, smartphone, or smart card, and something the user is, such as biometric data. Each factor plays a crucial role in enhancing the security of server access. For example, the most common form of MFA involves combining a password with an OTP sent to the user's mobile device. This combination ensures that even if a password is compromised, the attacker would still need the user's physical device to gain access.

Another important consideration when implementing MFA is ensuring that it integrates seamlessly with the existing authentication infrastructure and systems. Many modern server environments, particularly those running on Linux or Windows, already support MFA through third-party software or services. Some solutions can be easily integrated into existing directory services, such as Microsoft Active Directory or Lightweight Directory Access Protocol (LDAP), allowing MFA to be enforced at the authentication point for all users accessing the server. By configuring the server to require MFA for all remote and local access, organizations can ensure that every entry point is secured with an additional layer of authentication.

While the implementation of MFA significantly strengthens security, it is also important to ensure that the MFA solution is user-friendly and does not introduce unnecessary complexity. One of the key challenges with MFA is striking the right balance between security and usability. If the MFA process is too cumbersome or time-consuming, users may be tempted to bypass it, undermining the very security it is designed to provide. Therefore, it is essential to choose an MFA solution that is both effective and easy to use. For example, push notifications sent to a user's smartphone or an OTP sent via SMS or email are typically more user-friendly than requiring the user to input a code from a physical hardware token. Similarly, biometric authentication, such as fingerprint or facial recognition, provides a seamless experience without requiring the user to remember passwords or enter complex codes.

For organizations with a diverse workforce, it is important to offer flexible MFA options that accommodate different user needs and preferences. Some users may be more comfortable with hardware tokens or smart cards, while others may prefer using mobile apps for authentication. By offering multiple MFA methods, such as time-based OTPs generated by apps like Google Authenticator or Duo Mobile, or hardware tokens like YubiKey, organizations can ensure that users have access to the method that works best for them. This flexibility can help improve user adoption rates and compliance with the MFA policy, ensuring that all users benefit from the added security.

MFA is particularly critical for remote access to servers, as remote connections are often more vulnerable to attack. With the increasing use of remote work solutions and virtual private networks (VPNs), securing remote access to servers is a top priority. VPNs provide secure communication channels between remote users and internal networks, but without MFA, these connections can still be vulnerable to credential theft or compromise. By requiring MFA for all remote access, organizations ensure that even if an attacker obtains a user's login credentials, they cannot gain unauthorized access without the second factor. This added layer of protection is particularly important for organizations that manage servers containing sensitive data or mission-critical applications.

In addition to securing remote access, MFA is essential for protecting administrative access to servers. Server administrators often have privileged access to critical system functions, including user account management, system configurations, and application settings. If an attacker gains access to an administrator's account, they can potentially compromise the entire server. Therefore, enforcing MFA for administrative accounts ensures that even if an attacker manages to steal an administrator's password, they cannot perform critical actions without the second authentication factor. This is especially important in environments where administrators have full control over the server's configuration and can potentially introduce vulnerabilities or make unauthorized changes.

Implementing MFA also helps organizations meet compliance requirements for data protection and privacy regulations. Many regulations, such as the General Data Protection Regulation (GDPR), Health Insurance Portability and Accountability Act (HIPAA), and Payment Card Industry Data Security Standard (PCI DSS), mandate strong authentication practices to protect sensitive data. By enforcing MFA, organizations can demonstrate that they are taking the necessary steps to secure access to critical systems and protect user data. In addition, MFA helps organizations mitigate the risk of fines or penalties associated with non-compliance, as regulators often look favorably on organizations that implement multi-layered security measures to protect sensitive information.

While MFA offers significant security benefits, it is important for organizations to have a clear plan for managing the MFA solution over time. This includes ensuring that MFA methods are properly maintained and that users' devices are up to date with the latest security patches. As new authentication technologies emerge, organizations should continually assess the effectiveness of their MFA solution and make necessary adjustments. For example, organizations may decide to adopt biometric authentication, such as facial recognition or fingerprint scanning, as newer and more secure alternatives to traditional OTPs. Additionally, organizations should establish a process for dealing with lost or compromised MFA tokens, ensuring that users can quickly regain access without compromising security.

Incorporating MFA into server access not only provides a significant boost to security but also fosters a culture of proactive risk management. By requiring users to authenticate using multiple factors, organizations are effectively reducing the chances of unauthorized access and protecting against a wide range of cyber threats. As cyberattacks continue to evolve and become more sophisticated, adopting MFA is a critical step in staying ahead of attackers and ensuring that sensitive data and systems remain secure. Through the use of MFA, organizations can bolster the security of their server infrastructure and enhance their overall cybersecurity posture.

Securing Cloud Servers: Special Considerations

The adoption of cloud computing has transformed how organizations manage and store their data, offering unparalleled scalability, flexibility, and cost-efficiency. However, the very nature of cloud environments—where resources are shared, dynamic, and often geographically dispersed—introduces unique security challenges that must be addressed to ensure the protection of cloud servers and the data they host. Unlike traditional on-premise servers, cloud servers are typically hosted and maintained by third-party providers, which means organizations must rely on these providers to implement physical security and some aspects of network security. While cloud service providers (CSPs) typically offer robust security features, organizations must still take responsibility for securing their own cloud-based infrastructure. This shared responsibility model necessitates a nuanced approach to securing cloud servers, incorporating both technical measures and best practices that address the inherent risks associated with cloud computing.

One of the primary concerns when securing cloud servers is ensuring the proper configuration of the cloud environment. Misconfigurations are among the leading causes of data breaches in cloud environments. Cloud servers often provide a great deal of flexibility, allowing users to configure virtual machines, storage, networking, and access controls according to their specific needs. However, this flexibility can also lead to errors that open up security vulnerabilities. For example, cloud servers may inadvertently be exposed to the internet due to improperly configured access control lists (ACLs), or sensitive data may be stored in an unsecured, publicly accessible bucket in object storage.

Therefore, it is critical to implement strong configuration management practices to prevent such mistakes. Organizations must ensure that cloud instances are set up with the minimum necessary access and services, ensuring that unnecessary ports are closed and that default configurations are reviewed and hardened. Automated configuration management tools can help ensure consistency and compliance with best practices across all cloud resources.

Identity and access management (IAM) is another critical area of focus when securing cloud servers. In a cloud environment, organizations must implement robust IAM policies to control who has access to what resources and to ensure that access is granted based on the principle of least privilege. IAM in the cloud allows organizations to define roles and permissions, controlling which users, groups, or services have access to specific cloud resources. It is essential to enforce strong authentication mechanisms, such as multi-factor authentication (MFA), for users accessing cloud servers. This reduces the risk of unauthorized access, even if an attacker manages to steal login credentials. Additionally, organizations should adopt the practice of regularly reviewing access logs and conducting periodic access audits to ensure that users and services are not granted more privileges than necessary. Automated tools that monitor and alert for unusual access patterns or privilege escalation attempts can help detect potential security incidents before they escalate into full-blown breaches.

Data security is a fundamental concern for any cloud server deployment. In the cloud, data is often transmitted and stored outside the organization's direct control, making it susceptible to unauthorized access. To mitigate this risk, encryption should be used to protect sensitive data both in transit and at rest. Data encryption ensures that even if an attacker gains unauthorized access to cloud storage, they cannot read or manipulate the data without the decryption key. Cloud service providers often offer built-in encryption features, but organizations must ensure that encryption is properly configured and that keys are managed securely. For instance, using an external key management service (KMS) allows organizations to control and rotate encryption keys independently of the cloud provider, adding an additional layer of security. Furthermore, organizations should consider encrypting not only the most sensitive data but also less critical information, as a breach of any data can lead to greater security concerns.

Network security is another vital aspect of securing cloud servers. In cloud environments, servers are typically connected to one another through virtual networks, making it essential to secure these internal communication channels. Virtual private networks (VPNs) can be used to encrypt communications between cloud resources and between cloud servers and on-premise infrastructure. Firewalls and network segmentation should also be configured to isolate cloud servers and applications based on their roles and sensitivity. For example, production systems that handle customer data should be separated from development environments, which may not have the same level of security controls. Network security tools provided by the cloud provider, such as intrusion detection and prevention systems (IDPS), can also be leveraged to monitor for suspicious activity within the cloud environment and prevent attacks before they can penetrate deeper into the infrastructure.

A significant consideration when securing cloud servers is the management of server updates and patches. Cloud servers, like traditional servers, rely on operating system and application updates to patch vulnerabilities and improve security. However, in the cloud, the responsibility for applying updates may vary depending on the service model—whether it is Infrastructure as a Service (IaaS), Platform as a Service (PaaS), or Software as a Service (SaaS). For IaaS environments, organizations must ensure that their virtual machines and applications are regularly patched and that vulnerabilities are addressed promptly. Cloud service providers typically handle patching for the underlying physical infrastructure, but customers are still responsible for securing the software layer. In a PaaS environment, the provider manages the underlying software, but the organization is still responsible for patching any custom applications they develop. Maintaining an effective patch management policy and applying patches as soon as they are released is essential for minimizing exposure to known threats.

Backup and disaster recovery planning are also essential components of securing cloud servers. Despite the inherent reliability and redundancy of cloud infrastructure, data loss or server failure can still occur due to human error, software bugs, or malicious attacks. Cloud providers often offer backup services, but organizations should not rely solely on these services and should implement their own backup strategies. Data backups should be encrypted and stored in separate geographic regions to provide resilience in case of regional outages or disasters. A robust disaster recovery plan should define procedures for restoring data and services in the event of an outage, ensuring that business operations can resume quickly with minimal data loss. Regular testing of recovery procedures is crucial to ensure that they work effectively when needed.

Compliance with industry regulations and standards is another critical aspect of securing cloud servers. Cloud environments must comply with various data protection laws, such as the GDPR, HIPAA, or PCI DSS, depending on the nature of the data being stored or processed. These regulations often impose specific requirements related to data storage, access control, encryption, and incident reporting. Organizations must ensure that their cloud servers are configured to meet the requirements of these regulations, and this may involve working closely with cloud service providers to understand the shared responsibility model and ensure compliance.

In addition to these security measures, organizations should stay informed about the latest threats and vulnerabilities affecting cloud environments. As cloud computing continues to evolve, new attack vectors and vulnerabilities emerge. Organizations must maintain a proactive security posture, regularly updating their security policies, conducting vulnerability assessments, and adapting to new risks as they arise. Leveraging threat intelligence feeds and collaborating with the security community can help organizations stay ahead of evolving threats and protect their cloud infrastructure.

Securing cloud servers involves a multifaceted approach that encompasses configuration management, data security, access control, network security, patch management, and compliance. By implementing these best practices and utilizing the tools and services available from cloud providers, organizations can significantly reduce the risk of security breaches and ensure the safety of their critical systems and data in the cloud. Effective cloud server security requires ongoing vigilance and adaptation to new threats, but with the right strategies in place, organizations can leverage the power and flexibility of cloud computing while maintaining a strong security posture.

The Role of Security Automation in System Hardening

As cyber threats continue to evolve and become more sophisticated, organizations are increasingly turning to security automation as a means to enhance their system hardening efforts. System hardening refers to the process of securing a system by reducing its vulnerabilities, often through the configuration of security settings and the removal of unnecessary services. While traditional manual methods of system hardening can be effective, they are often time-consuming, prone to human error, and difficult to scale across large and complex environments. Security automation, on the other hand, offers a way to streamline and accelerate the hardening process, ensuring that security measures are consistently applied across systems, even in highly dynamic and distributed environments. By automating critical security tasks, organizations can strengthen their defenses, reduce the risk of configuration errors, and maintain a more resilient infrastructure.

One of the primary benefits of security automation in system hardening is the ability to consistently enforce security policies across all systems in an organization. With manual processes, there is always the possibility of oversight or error, particularly when managing a large number of systems. A misconfigured system can be a prime target for cyberattacks, as attackers often exploit configuration weaknesses to gain unauthorized access. Security automation tools can ensure that security policies, such as password strength requirements, encryption settings, and network configurations, are uniformly applied across the entire system infrastructure. This reduces the chances of vulnerabilities slipping through the cracks and ensures that all systems are hardened to the same standards, regardless of their individual configurations or the personnel managing them.

Security automation can also help organizations keep systems up to date with the latest security patches and updates. One of the most common causes of system breaches is the failure to apply patches in a timely manner. Cybercriminals often exploit known vulnerabilities in software that have already been patched, but if those patches are not applied promptly, the system remains vulnerable. Manual patching can be a cumbersome process, especially in large environments where many systems need to be updated. With automation, patches can be applied automatically and consistently across all systems as soon as they are released, reducing the risk of exploits. Moreover, automation can help organizations prioritize patching based on the severity of the vulnerabilities, ensuring that the most critical updates are applied first. This reduces the window of opportunity for attackers to exploit unpatched vulnerabilities.

Another key advantage of security automation is its ability to provide continuous monitoring and auditing of system configurations. Traditional methods of system hardening typically involve a one-time configuration followed by periodic audits to ensure compliance. However, this approach can leave gaps in security, as systems may change over time, and new vulnerabilities may emerge. Security automation tools, on the other hand, can continuously monitor systems for deviations from established security baselines, ensuring that any changes to configurations are detected in real-time. For example, if a user accidentally disables a critical firewall rule or opens an unnecessary network port, automation tools can detect these changes and alert administrators or automatically remediate the issue. This ongoing monitoring helps maintain a hardened system and ensures that security settings are always aligned with organizational policies.

Automation also plays a critical role in vulnerability management, which is an essential component of system hardening. In a dynamic environment, vulnerabilities can be introduced at any time, whether due to software updates, configuration changes, or new attack vectors. Security automation tools can integrate with vulnerability management systems to automatically scan for known vulnerabilities and misconfigurations. These tools can prioritize vulnerabilities based on risk and impact, providing administrators with a clear overview of the most critical issues that need to be addressed. Additionally, security automation can facilitate the patching of known vulnerabilities or the implementation of mitigations without manual intervention, accelerating the response time to emerging threats. By automating vulnerability management, organizations can reduce their exposure to known threats and ensure that their systems remain up to date with the latest security patches.

Another benefit of security automation is the reduction of human error. Even the most experienced administrators can make mistakes, especially when manually configuring security settings across large, complex systems. These errors can introduce vulnerabilities that are difficult to detect and may remain unnoticed until an attack occurs. Automation minimizes the risk of human error by ensuring that security configurations are applied in a consistent, repeatable manner. Furthermore, automated tools can provide detailed logs and reports, which help administrators track changes, monitor compliance, and investigate potential security incidents. This audit trail can be invaluable for identifying the root cause of issues and improving future security practices.

Automation can also help organizations respond more effectively to security incidents. In the event of a breach or attempted attack, time is of the essence. Security automation tools can help organizations respond to incidents quickly by automatically implementing predefined remediation actions, such as blocking malicious IP addresses, isolating compromised systems, or restoring secure configurations. This reduces the time it takes to contain and mitigate threats, minimizing potential damage. Automation can also assist with incident response planning by simulating attack scenarios and testing the effectiveness of response procedures. This allows organizations to refine their response strategies and ensure that they are well-prepared for real-world attacks.

Moreover, security automation supports compliance with regulatory standards and frameworks. Many industries are subject to strict security regulations, such as HIPAA, PCI DSS, or GDPR, which require organizations to implement specific security measures and maintain detailed records of compliance. Security automation can help organizations adhere to these regulations by ensuring that security settings are consistently applied and that audits are conducted regularly. Automated tools can generate compliance reports, track security metrics, and provide documentation to demonstrate that security controls are in place and functioning as required by regulatory standards. By streamlining the compliance process, automation reduces the administrative burden on security teams and helps organizations avoid penalties for non-compliance.

Security automation is particularly useful in cloud environments, where the dynamic nature of cloud infrastructure can make it challenging to maintain consistent security configurations. Cloud environments often involve multiple servers, networks, and applications that are provisioned and decommissioned on demand. Automation tools can help organizations maintain a secure configuration across these dynamic resources by automatically applying security policies whenever new resources are spun up or old ones are decommissioned. This ensures that security controls are enforced consistently across the entire cloud environment, regardless of the scale or complexity of the infrastructure.

Implementing security automation also supports scalability, enabling organizations to expand their infrastructure without sacrificing security. As organizations grow and add more servers, applications, and users, manual hardening efforts become increasingly difficult to manage. Automation allows organizations to scale their security practices to match the growth of their infrastructure. By automating routine security tasks, such as applying patches, configuring firewalls, and auditing system configurations, organizations can manage larger, more complex systems with fewer resources and greater efficiency.

Security automation is a powerful tool for enhancing system hardening efforts by streamlining configuration management, patching, vulnerability management, and incident response. By automating security processes, organizations can reduce human error, accelerate response times, and ensure consistent implementation of security controls across their infrastructure. As cyber threats continue to grow in complexity, security automation will become an increasingly vital component of an effective cybersecurity strategy, enabling organizations to maintain a resilient and secure environment in the face of ever-evolving risks.

Container Security: Best Practices for Docker and Kubernetes

Containerization technology has revolutionized the way applications are developed, deployed, and managed. With Docker and Kubernetes leading the way, containers provide a lightweight, portable, and efficient way to package applications and their dependencies, allowing them to run consistently across various environments. However, the use of containers introduces new security challenges, as the traditional security models used for virtual machines and physical servers do not necessarily apply. Ensuring the security of containers, particularly in production environments, requires a comprehensive approach that includes both securing the container images themselves and properly configuring the orchestration platforms like Kubernetes. Best practices for container security involve a combination of strategies aimed at securing the entire container lifecycle—from development and image creation to deployment, runtime, and monitoring.

One of the first steps in securing containers is to focus on the security of the container images. A container image is essentially a snapshot of an application and its dependencies, so it is critical to ensure that these images are free from vulnerabilities before they are deployed. Using base images from trusted sources is essential to reducing the risk of introducing malicious code. Public repositories, such as Docker Hub, contain a wide range of pre-built images, but not all of these images are secure or maintained with security patches. Organizations should use only official or trusted images and verify their integrity before use. Additionally, image scanning tools can be used to automatically detect vulnerabilities within container images. These tools analyze the contents of an image and identify known vulnerabilities, such as outdated libraries or insecure configurations, which could be exploited by attackers.

Once an image is deemed secure, the next step is to ensure that containers are run with the principle of least privilege. This means that containers should be granted the minimum amount of access necessary to perform their functions. One of the advantages of containerization is its ability to isolate applications from one another and from the underlying host system. However, misconfigurations can result in overly permissive settings that allow containers to gain unnecessary access to the host system, other containers, or sensitive data. For example, running a container with root privileges should be avoided, as this could allow an attacker who compromises the container to gain full control of the host system. Instead, containers should be run with non-root users whenever possible, and the necessary permissions should be granted based on the principle of least privilege.

Another critical aspect of securing containers is securing their communication with other containers and services. Containers often need to communicate with each other and with external services, but unencrypted communication can expose sensitive data to interception. To address this, communication between containers should be encrypted, and secure protocols should be used. In Kubernetes, for instance, service-to-service communication can be secured using mutual TLS (Transport Layer Security), ensuring that only authorized services are allowed to communicate with each other. Additionally, network policies can be used to control traffic flow between containers, limiting access based on the container's role within the application architecture. For example, a container running a front-end application should not have direct access to databases unless explicitly required.

In Kubernetes, ensuring the security of the orchestration platform itself is equally important. Kubernetes provides powerful features for container orchestration and management, but without proper configuration, these features can become security risks. One key consideration is securing the Kubernetes API server, which is the control plane for managing and scheduling containers. The API server is a critical component, and any vulnerability here can lead to the compromise of the entire cluster. To mitigate this, access to the Kubernetes API server should be tightly controlled using role-based access control (RBAC) to enforce least privilege for users and service accounts. Additionally, securing the communication between components within the Kubernetes cluster is essential. All communication should be encrypted using TLS, and authentication should be enforced using certificates or other secure methods.

Another important best practice is to manage and monitor containerized environments continuously. Containers are dynamic by nature, and new instances can be spun up and shut down at any time. This dynamic nature can make it difficult to track vulnerabilities and ensure that security policies are consistently applied across all containers. Kubernetes provides features such as Kubernetes Audit Logs and monitoring tools like Prometheus and Grafana, which can be used to track container activity and detect anomalous behavior in real-time. These tools help security teams identify potential security incidents early and take corrective action before any significant damage occurs. Moreover, integrating security into the continuous integration/continuous deployment (CI/CD) pipeline ensures that security checks are performed automatically whenever a new container image is built or updated, ensuring that vulnerabilities are identified and addressed before deployment.

Container runtime security is also a key consideration in securing containerized environments. The container runtime is responsible for starting and managing containers on the host system. A common container runtime is Docker, but other options, such as containerd and CRI-O, are available in Kubernetes environments. Securing the container runtime involves ensuring that the runtime is updated regularly to address security vulnerabilities and that proper configuration settings are applied to restrict the capabilities of containers. For example, using security profiles such as AppArmor or SELinux (Security-Enhanced Linux) can help restrict container behaviors and prevent them from accessing unauthorized resources. These profiles define security policies that control what containers can do and access, adding an additional layer of protection to the runtime environment.

Additionally, container registries must be secured to prevent the introduction of malicious code into the container supply chain. A container registry is where container images are stored before deployment, and like container images themselves, registries can be vulnerable to attacks. Using private container registries with appropriate access controls ensures that only authorized users and systems can push or pull images. Furthermore, ensuring that the images in the registry are scanned for vulnerabilities before deployment helps prevent the use of insecure or outdated images in production environments.

A robust incident response plan is essential for dealing with security incidents involving containers. Containers can be quickly spun up and spun down, which makes it harder to trace and respond to attacks if the environment is not properly monitored. In the event of a breach or suspected security incident, organizations should have processes in place to identify compromised containers, isolate them from the rest of the environment, and conduct forensic investigations. Regularly testing the incident response plan, particularly in a containerized environment, ensures that security teams can act quickly and efficiently when incidents occur.

The final layer of security involves securing the underlying host system that runs the containers. Even though containers are designed to isolate applications from the host system, vulnerabilities in the host system can still affect the entire container environment. Keeping the host operating system updated, using secure configurations, and reducing the number of unnecessary services running on the host are all essential steps in securing the environment. Using specialized security tools like Docker's content trust and tools for securing Kubernetes nodes helps ensure that the host system remains secure and resilient to attacks.

Securing containerized environments is an ongoing process that requires continuous attention and adaptation to new threats. By following best practices such as securing container images, limiting privileges, encrypting communication, securing Kubernetes configurations, and maintaining strong runtime security, organizations can create a more secure container infrastructure. Continuous monitoring and integration of security into the CI/CD pipeline will help detect vulnerabilities early and ensure that containers are deployed with strong security controls. As containerization continues to grow in popularity, securing container environments will remain a critical element of an organization's overall security strategy.

Securing Server Communication with VPNs

In today's interconnected world, securing communication between servers is a fundamental aspect of maintaining a secure IT infrastructure. Servers often need to exchange sensitive data over the internet or private networks, and without proper protection, this data can be intercepted or tampered with by malicious actors. Virtual Private Networks (VPNs) offer an effective solution to this challenge, providing a secure tunnel through which data can be transmitted safely, even across untrusted networks. VPNs are widely used in server-to-server communication, especially in cloud environments, remote access scenarios, and multi-location deployments. By ensuring that server communication is encrypted and authenticated, VPNs help protect the integrity, confidentiality, and privacy of data, preventing unauthorized access and potential security breaches.

A VPN works by creating an encrypted tunnel between two endpoints, often between a server and a client or between two servers, over a public network such as the internet. This tunnel encrypts all data passing through it, making it unreadable to anyone intercepting the traffic. The encryption ensures that even if an attacker manages to capture the data, it remains protected and unusable without the correct decryption keys. In addition to encryption, VPNs also use authentication mechanisms to verify the identities of the communicating parties. This ensures that only authorized users or systems can establish a connection, further enhancing the security of server communication.

When configuring a VPN for server communication, it is important to select a protocol that provides strong encryption and security features. There are several VPN protocols to choose from, each offering different levels of security and performance. For example, OpenVPN is a widely used protocol known for its strong encryption capabilities and flexibility, while IPsec (Internet Protocol Security) is often used in enterprise environments for its ability to secure communication at the network layer. Other protocols, such as L2TP (Layer 2 Tunneling Protocol) and PPTP (Point-to-Point Tunneling Protocol), may be used in specific scenarios but are generally considered less secure compared to OpenVPN or IPsec. The choice of protocol depends on the specific requirements of the environment, such as the need for high-performance communication, compatibility with existing infrastructure, and the level of security required for the data being transmitted.

One of the key benefits of using VPNs for server communication is that they help protect data from interception and man-in-the-middle (MITM) attacks. MITM attacks occur when an attacker intercepts the communication between two systems and potentially alters or steals the data being transmitted. Without a VPN, server communication over public networks, such as the internet, is susceptible to such attacks. By encrypting the traffic, VPNs ensure that even if an attacker intercepts the data, they cannot read or modify it without the proper decryption keys. This protection is particularly important when servers are communicating across public networks, where the risk of interception is high. In addition, VPNs can also prevent eavesdropping by obfuscating the communication, making it difficult for unauthorized parties to identify the source or destination of the traffic.

Authentication is another crucial aspect of securing server communication with VPNs. A VPN connection is only as secure as the authentication methods used to verify the identity of the servers involved. In a server-to-server communication scenario, strong mutual authentication should be implemented, ensuring that both servers can verify each other's identities before exchanging data. This is typically achieved through the use of digital certificates, pre-shared keys (PSKs), or a combination of both. Digital certificates, often issued by a trusted certificate authority (CA), provide a way to authenticate servers using public key infrastructure (PKI). By requiring servers to present valid certificates, organizations can ensure that only authorized servers are able to establish a connection. Additionally, pre-shared keys (PSKs) can be used as an alternative or supplementary authentication method, where both servers agree on a shared secret key before initiating the VPN connection.

In addition to authentication and encryption, VPNs also provide integrity checks to ensure that the data sent between servers is not tampered with during transmission. This is typically done through the use of hash algorithms, which generate a unique hash value for each packet of data. When the data is received by the other server, the hash is recalculated and compared to the original hash value to verify that the data has not been altered. This integrity check helps ensure that data is not corrupted or modified by attackers while in transit, providing an additional layer of protection to the communication process.

While VPNs offer strong security for server-to-server communication, proper configuration and ongoing maintenance are essential to maximizing their effectiveness. One common mistake when implementing VPNs is the use of weak encryption algorithms or poorly configured authentication mechanisms. Organizations must ensure that their VPNs are using strong encryption methods, such as AES (Advanced Encryption Standard), which provides robust protection against brute-force attacks. Additionally, VPNs should be configured to use secure key exchange algorithms, such as Diffie-Hellman or Elliptic Curve Diffie-Hellman, to ensure that encryption keys are exchanged securely during the handshake process. Weak or default passwords for VPN accounts should be avoided, and strong password policies should be enforced to prevent unauthorized access.

Another important consideration when securing server communication with VPNs is the management of VPN credentials. Over time, credentials may need to be updated or revoked, particularly when users or servers are decommissioned or if security breaches occur. Automating the process of managing VPN credentials can help ensure that only authorized users and servers have access to the network. Regularly rotating VPN keys and updating authentication certificates are essential practices to prevent credential leakage and mitigate the risk of unauthorized access. Organizations should also establish procedures for revoking access to compromised or obsolete credentials, ensuring that security is maintained even when changes occur in the network.

When deploying VPNs for server communication, organizations should also consider performance implications. VPN encryption and decryption processes require computational resources, and excessive use of VPN connections can impact the performance of the servers and the overall network. It is essential to balance security with performance by optimizing the VPN configuration and ensuring that the VPN solution can scale to meet the organization's needs. Choosing the right VPN protocol and encryption method can help minimize the performance impact without compromising security. Load balancing techniques and redundant VPN connections can also be used to ensure that traffic is efficiently distributed and that the VPN infrastructure remains resilient during high-demand periods.

In large-scale environments, where multiple servers are involved in complex communication patterns, the use of a dedicated VPN appliance or a VPN service provider may be necessary to manage the growing number of connections. These appliances and services are designed to handle large volumes of encrypted traffic and provide additional features such as centralized logging, threat detection, and monitoring capabilities. By offloading VPN management to a specialized service, organizations can focus on securing their infrastructure while benefiting from the expertise of VPN providers in maintaining high levels of security and performance.

VPNs are a crucial tool for securing server communication in modern IT environments. They provide a reliable and efficient way to encrypt data, authenticate servers, and ensure the integrity of communications. By implementing best practices such as using strong encryption, configuring secure authentication methods, and managing VPN credentials effectively, organizations can protect their server infrastructure from a wide range of cyber threats. With the growing complexity of network environments and the increasing reliance on cloud services and remote access, VPNs continue to play an essential role in securing server communication and maintaining the integrity of sensitive data as it travels across networks.

Preventing and Mitigating SQL Injection Attacks

SQL injection is one of the most common and dangerous types of web application vulnerabilities. It occurs when an attacker is able to insert malicious SQL code into a query, allowing them to manipulate or access a database in unintended ways. The consequences of SQL injection attacks can be devastating, including unauthorized access to sensitive data, modification or deletion of data, and in some cases, complete system compromise. SQL injection attacks take advantage of weaknesses in the way web applications interact with databases, and they can be carried out with minimal technical knowledge, making them a significant threat to organizations of all sizes. Preventing and mitigating SQL injection attacks requires a combination of secure coding practices, proactive testing, and the proper configuration of database access controls.

SQL injection attacks typically occur when user input is improperly sanitized or validated before being used in SQL queries. In vulnerable applications, user input is incorporated directly into SQL statements without adequate checking, allowing an attacker to inject arbitrary SQL code that the database will execute. For example, an attacker might enter SQL code into a login form that manipulates the query, bypassing authentication or retrieving unauthorized data. The risk is even greater in applications that provide insufficient error handling or detailed error messages, as these can reveal information about the structure of the database and assist attackers in crafting more precise injection attacks.

The first step in preventing SQL injection attacks is to avoid directly concatenating user input into SQL queries. This is a fundamental mistake that allows attackers to manipulate the SQL query to perform unauthorized actions. Instead, developers should use parameterized queries or prepared statements, which separate the query logic from the user input. In parameterized queries, the SQL query is predefined, and placeholders are used to represent user input. The user input is then passed separately to the database engine, which ensures that the input is treated as data, not executable code. This technique eliminates the risk of injection, as the user input cannot alter the structure of the query. Most modern database libraries and frameworks support parameterized queries, making them an essential tool in defending against SQL injection.

Another important practice in preventing SQL injection attacks is the proper validation and sanitization of user input. All data submitted by users, including form inputs, query parameters, and cookies, should be treated as untrusted. Developers should enforce strict validation rules that ensure only valid input is accepted. For example, if a form expects a user's email address, the input should be validated to ensure that it matches the expected format. If the input includes characters or patterns that are not allowed in the context of the application, such as SQL keywords or special characters, it should be rejected or sanitized before being used in SQL queries. Input sanitization involves removing or escaping special characters that could be interpreted as part of an SQL command, further reducing the risk of injection. It is important to note that input sanitization should not be relied upon as the primary defense mechanism; instead, it should be used in conjunction with parameterized queries to provide layered protection.

Limiting the database permissions granted to web applications is another key strategy for mitigating the impact of SQL injection attacks. If an attacker successfully exploits an SQL injection vulnerability, the damage they can cause depends on the level of access the application has to the database. To minimize the potential harm, web applications should be granted the least amount of privilege necessary to perform their intended tasks. For example, if an application only needs to read data from a database, it should not be granted write or delete permissions. By implementing strict access controls and following the principle of least privilege, organizations can limit the scope of what an attacker can do, even if they manage to exploit an SQL injection vulnerability.

Error handling is another area where SQL injection risks can be mitigated. Detailed error messages that reveal information about the underlying database or SQL queries should never be displayed to end users. These error messages can provide attackers with valuable information about the structure of the database, including table names, column names, and other details that can aid in crafting more sophisticated attacks. Instead, generic error messages should be used, and all detailed error information should be logged for internal review by administrators. This ensures that attackers are not provided with the information they need to exploit vulnerabilities, while still allowing security teams to investigate and address issues.

In addition to secure coding practices, regular testing and security assessments are crucial for identifying and addressing SQL injection vulnerabilities. One of the most effective ways to detect SQL injection flaws is through penetration testing, in which ethical hackers attempt to exploit vulnerabilities in the application's SQL queries. Penetration testing can help uncover weak points in the application and provide valuable insights into how an attacker might exploit them. Automated vulnerability scanning tools can also be used to detect common SQL injection patterns in web applications. These tools can scan an application's input points and attempt to inject SQL payloads, identifying potential vulnerabilities that need to be addressed.

Web application firewalls (WAFs) can also provide an additional layer of defense against SQL injection attacks. WAFs are designed to filter and monitor HTTP traffic between a web server and its users, inspecting incoming requests for malicious payloads and blocking those that appear suspicious. Many WAFs come equipped with rules and signatures specifically designed to detect SQL injection attempts, and they can provide real-time protection against common attack vectors. While WAFs should not be relied upon as the sole defense mechanism, they can be an effective tool for complementing other security measures, especially in environments where application-level changes are difficult to implement.

Database-level security features can also help mitigate the impact of SQL injection attacks. For example, many database systems provide features like query whitelisting, which allows administrators to define a set of safe queries that are allowed to run while blocking others. This can help prevent unauthorized SQL commands from being executed, even if they are injected through a vulnerable application. Additionally, database systems should be configured to log all queries, enabling administrators to detect suspicious activity and investigate potential injection attempts. Logging can help identify patterns of attack, such as repeated attempts to exploit a particular vulnerability, and provide valuable information for improving defenses.

Organizations should also educate their developers and security teams on the risks of SQL injection and the importance of secure coding practices. Developers should be trained on the proper techniques for preventing SQL injection, such as using parameterized queries, validating input, and handling errors securely. Security teams should be involved in the development lifecycle, performing regular code reviews and vulnerability scans to ensure that SQL injection risks are addressed early in the development process. Building security into the development process, often referred to as "secure by design," can significantly reduce the likelihood of vulnerabilities being introduced in the first place.

SQL injection is a persistent and dangerous threat to web applications, but with the right security measures in place, organizations can greatly reduce the risk of successful attacks. By using parameterized queries, validating and sanitizing user input, restricting database permissions, and employing proper error handling, developers can secure their applications from SQL injection. Regular testing, combined with web application firewalls and database-level security features, provides an additional layer of protection. With a proactive, defense-in-depth approach, organizations can protect their systems from the destructive effects of SQL injection and safeguard their sensitive data from attackers.

Hardening DNS Servers Against Common Vulnerabilities

Domain Name System (DNS) servers are fundamental components of the internet infrastructure, serving as the address book for the internet by translating human-readable domain names into IP addresses that computers use to communicate. As essential as DNS is for the functioning of networks, DNS servers are also prime targets for attackers looking to exploit vulnerabilities for malicious purposes. Given their critical role in network communication, DNS servers must be properly secured to prevent unauthorized access, data manipulation, and service disruptions. Hardening DNS servers against common vulnerabilities is essential to ensure the availability, confidentiality, and integrity of both internal and external network traffic.

One of the primary vulnerabilities that DNS servers face is DNS spoofing, also known as DNS cache poisoning. This attack occurs when an attacker inserts false DNS records into a server's cache, leading it to resolve domain names to incorrect IP addresses. For example, a user trying to visit a legitimate website might be redirected to a malicious website without their knowledge. To mitigate the risk of DNS spoofing, it is essential to use DNSSEC (Domain Name System Security Extensions), a security protocol designed to protect against such attacks. DNSSEC adds a layer of cryptographic authentication to DNS responses, ensuring that the data received by the server has not been tampered with. By signing DNS data with cryptographic signatures, DNSSEC helps ensure the integrity and authenticity of the DNS responses, making it far more difficult for attackers to inject malicious information into DNS queries.

Another significant vulnerability that DNS servers face is denial-of-service (DoS) attacks, which aim to overwhelm the server with a flood of requests, causing it to become unresponsive. One of the most common forms of DNS-related DoS attacks is the amplification attack. In this attack, the attacker exploits vulnerable DNS servers to send a massive amount of traffic to a target server, often using spoofed IP addresses to hide their identity. To defend against such attacks, DNS servers should be configured to limit the size of response packets and use rate-limiting techniques to prevent abuse. Additionally, DNS servers should be configured to prevent recursion for external users, ensuring that DNS servers only provide resolutions for domains within the local network and do not act as open resolvers that can be abused by attackers.

Additionally, ensuring that DNS servers are properly configured to handle access control is critical for hardening the server. Unauthorized access to DNS configuration files or administrative interfaces can lead to significant security issues. For example, an attacker with administrative access to a DNS server could modify records, redirect traffic, or disrupt services. It is essential to implement strict access control policies, allowing only authorized personnel to access the server configuration and management interfaces. Network segmentation can be used to isolate DNS servers from other internal services, limiting the attack surface and minimizing the potential for unauthorized access. Furthermore, DNS management interfaces should be protected by strong authentication methods, such as multi-factor authentication (MFA), to ensure that only legitimate administrators can make changes to the DNS settings.

Regular software updates and patch management are also crucial elements of securing DNS servers. Like any software, DNS server software can contain vulnerabilities that attackers may exploit. It is essential to regularly check for updates and security patches released by the software vendors to ensure that the server is protected from known exploits. Automatic patching tools can be used to keep the DNS software up to date, but administrators should also perform manual checks to confirm that the patches are applied correctly. Vulnerabilities that are not patched promptly may leave DNS servers exposed to a variety of attacks, including those that target known software weaknesses or misconfigurations.

In addition to applying patches, DNS servers should be configured to log and monitor all activity. Comprehensive logging helps administrators detect suspicious activity, such as unauthorized configuration changes or abnormal query patterns that may indicate a possible attack. DNS logs should include details on incoming queries, responses, errors, and any changes to DNS records. Monitoring tools can analyze these logs for signs of potential threats, such as a sudden spike in query volume, which may be indicative of a DoS attack, or unusual query patterns that may point to attempts at data exfiltration or reconnaissance. Regularly reviewing these logs allows administrators to identify and respond to security incidents more effectively.

Another important consideration in hardening DNS servers is the use of split-horizon DNS. This configuration involves maintaining separate DNS servers for internal and external requests. Internal DNS servers handle domain resolution requests for resources within the organization's network, while external DNS servers resolve requests for domains outside the network. This separation helps protect internal network structures from exposure to the internet, reducing the risk of data leaks or attacks that target internal resources. In addition to improving security, split-horizon DNS can enhance performance by allowing more efficient resolution of internal domain names and preventing unnecessary traffic from reaching external DNS servers.

To protect against DNS-related threats, DNS servers should also employ DNS query minimization. In traditional DNS queries, the DNS server may send large amounts of information back to the requesting client, some of which may be unnecessary or sensitive. DNS query minimization reduces the amount of data sent in response to queries, limiting the exposure of sensitive information. This minimizes the chances of an attacker gaining valuable information from a DNS query, such as the structure of a domain's records or internal network details. By only sending the necessary information, DNS query minimization helps reduce the potential attack surface and improves privacy.

One of the most important yet often overlooked aspects of DNS server security is the physical security of the server infrastructure. DNS servers are typically housed in data centers or server rooms, and securing these physical locations is just as critical as securing the server software itself. Unauthorized physical access to the server can lead to theft, tampering, or malicious modification of the system. Ensuring that DNS servers are stored in locked and monitored facilities, with access limited to authorized personnel, can significantly reduce the risk of physical attacks. In addition, data backups should be stored securely, and recovery procedures should be in place to restore the server to a known secure state in the event of a compromise.

Finally, implementing a robust incident response plan is essential for quickly addressing potential security incidents involving DNS servers. An effective incident response plan should outline the steps to take in the event of a DNS attack, such as isolating the affected servers, analyzing logs for indicators of compromise, and restoring service from secure backups. By regularly testing and updating the incident response plan, organizations can ensure that they are prepared to handle DNS-related security incidents promptly and effectively.

Securing DNS servers against common vulnerabilities requires a multi-layered approach that involves securing server configurations, monitoring activity, limiting access, and ensuring regular software updates. By implementing best practices such as using DNSSEC, enforcing access controls, and protecting against DoS attacks, organizations can significantly reduce the risk of successful attacks targeting DNS infrastructure. As DNS remains a critical component of modern network communication, maintaining the security and integrity of DNS servers is essential to the overall security of the IT environment. Through proactive measures and constant vigilance, organizations can protect their DNS infrastructure and ensure that it remains a reliable and secure part of their network infrastructure.

Securing Email Servers: Preventing Phishing and Spam

Email is one of the most widely used forms of communication in both personal and business environments. It is also one of the primary methods used by cybercriminals to carry out attacks, particularly phishing and spam campaigns. Phishing attacks aim to deceive recipients into revealing sensitive information, such as usernames, passwords, or financial details, by posing as a legitimate entity. Spam, on the other hand, consists of unsolicited emails that can clutter inboxes and often contain malicious attachments or links. Email servers, therefore, play a crucial role in preventing these threats, and securing email servers is essential for maintaining the confidentiality, integrity, and availability of an organization's communication infrastructure. By implementing a combination of technical measures, policies, and best practices, organizations can significantly reduce the risk of phishing and spam affecting their email systems.

One of the most effective ways to secure email servers against phishing and spam is to implement robust spam filtering mechanisms. These filters are designed to detect and block unwanted emails before they reach users' inboxes. Modern spam filters use a variety of techniques to identify spam, such as keyword analysis, blacklists, and Bayesian filters, which analyze the likelihood that an email is spam based on historical data. The filters also analyze the email's metadata, such as the sender's address, subject line, and message content, to detect patterns commonly associated with spam and phishing attempts. Additionally, spam filters can check if the sending server is on a known blacklist, which may indicate that it has been associated with malicious activity in the past. By filtering out spam and phishing emails at the server level, organizations can prevent these messages from reaching users and reduce the chances of a successful attack.

Another critical aspect of securing email servers is the use of strong email authentication protocols. Email authentication protocols, such as SPF (Sender Policy Framework), DKIM (DomainKeys Identified Mail), and DMARC (Domain-based Message Authentication,

Reporting & Conformance), are designed to verify that emails are sent from legitimate sources and not from malicious actors pretending to be trusted senders. SPF allows domain owners to specify which mail servers are authorized to send emails on behalf of their domain, helping to prevent email spoofing, where attackers forge the sender's address to make the email appear as though it came from a trusted source. DKIM uses digital signatures to verify the authenticity of the email, ensuring that the message has not been altered during transmission. DMARC builds on SPF and DKIM by allowing domain owners to specify how emails that fail authentication should be handled, whether they should be rejected or quarantined. Together, these protocols form a robust framework for email authentication that can help prevent phishing attacks that rely on email spoofing.

In addition to email authentication, organizations should employ transport layer security (TLS) to protect email communications in transit. TLS encrypts the connection between email servers, ensuring that emails are transmitted securely and cannot be intercepted by unauthorized third parties. Without encryption, emails can be intercepted or modified while in transit, which exposes them to potential attackers who can then steal sensitive information or inject malicious content. While many email services and servers support TLS by default, it is important to ensure that it is properly configured and that it is required for all incoming and outgoing email communications. This helps to safeguard both internal and external communications and adds an additional layer of protection against man-in-the-middle attacks.

Employee training is another crucial aspect of securing email servers and preventing phishing attacks. Despite the best technical defenses, phishing attacks can still succeed if users are not vigilant in recognizing suspicious emails. Cybercriminals are increasingly using social engineering tactics to craft convincing phishing emails that appear to come from trusted sources. These emails may contain links to fake websites that resemble legitimate ones or include attachments designed to deliver malware. Employees should be trained to recognize common signs of phishing attempts, such as unfamiliar sender addresses, generic subject lines, and requests for sensitive information. Regular training sessions, simulated phishing campaigns, and awareness programs can help users become more adept at identifying phishing attempts and reduce the likelihood of falling victim to these attacks.

A critical component of email server security is ensuring that email accounts are protected with strong, unique passwords and multi-factor authentication (MFA). Attackers often target weak or reused passwords to gain access to email accounts, which can be used to send phishing emails, steal sensitive information, or compromise other accounts linked to the email address. Enforcing password policies that require strong, complex passwords and using MFA adds an additional layer of security, making it significantly harder for attackers to gain unauthorized access to email accounts. With MFA enabled, even if an attacker manages to obtain a password, they would still need to pass an additional authentication step, such as a one-time passcode sent to the user's phone or a biometric scan, to access the account. This greatly reduces the effectiveness of credential-stuffing and brute-force attacks.

To further protect email servers from phishing and spam, organizations should implement regular vulnerability assessments and security patches for email server software. Like any other software, email server software can contain vulnerabilities that attackers can exploit to gain unauthorized access or launch attacks. Regularly updating email server software and applying security patches ensures that any known vulnerabilities are addressed before they can be exploited. In addition, email server configurations should be reviewed and hardened to prevent potential exploitation. This includes disabling unnecessary features, restricting access to the server's administration panel, and ensuring that the server is not configured to relay messages to unauthorized recipients.

Email servers should also be configured to prevent email forwarding to external or untrusted destinations. While email forwarding is a useful feature in many legitimate scenarios, it can also be exploited by attackers to bypass internal security measures and send phishing emails from trusted addresses. For example, if an attacker gains access to an employee's email account and configures it to forward emails to an external address, they could use that account to send phishing emails without detection. Restricting email forwarding and monitoring for unauthorized forwarding configurations helps prevent this type of abuse and ensures that sensitive internal communications remain secure.

Lastly, implementing a comprehensive incident response plan is essential for mitigating the effects of successful phishing attacks. Even with the best preventive measures in place, some phishing attempts may still succeed. Having a clear, well-documented incident response plan ensures that the organization can quickly respond to any phishing attack that bypasses technical defenses. This plan should include procedures for identifying compromised accounts, blocking phishing emails, restoring access to affected systems, and notifying impacted parties. Regularly testing and updating the incident response plan through tabletop exercises and real-world simulations helps ensure that the organization is prepared to handle phishing incidents efficiently and effectively.

Securing email servers against phishing and spam requires a multi-layered approach that combines technical defenses, such as email authentication and encryption, with proactive user training and awareness. By implementing these strategies, organizations can significantly reduce the risk of phishing attacks and ensure that their email systems remain secure. From strengthening server configurations to ensuring employee vigilance, each component plays a critical role in maintaining the security of email communication. Given the growing sophistication of phishing attacks, maintaining robust defenses against these threats is essential to protecting sensitive information and safeguarding the organization's reputation.

Implementing Web Application Firewalls (WAFs)

Web Application Firewalls (WAFs) are crucial security tools that help protect web applications from a wide range of threats and vulnerabilities. With the increasing sophistication of cyberattacks and the growing reliance on web-based services, web applications have become prime targets for attackers. These applications are vulnerable to a variety of attacks, such as SQL injection, cross-site scripting (XSS), and cross-site request forgery (CSRF). As web applications are critical to modern businesses, ensuring their security is of paramount importance. Implementing a WAF is an effective way to defend web applications from these common attacks by filtering and monitoring HTTP traffic between the web application and the internet.

WAFs are designed to inspect incoming traffic and identify potentially malicious requests before they reach the application itself. They work by analyzing HTTP/HTTPS requests for known attack patterns and blocking traffic that matches these patterns. A WAF typically sits between the client and the web server, acting as a reverse proxy to intercept and filter traffic. This position allows it to examine all incoming traffic, looking for signs of suspicious activity or known attack vectors. By filtering out harmful requests, a WAF helps prevent attackers from exploiting vulnerabilities in the application and ensures that only legitimate, non-malicious traffic reaches the web server.

One of the primary benefits of using a WAF is its ability to protect against common web application vulnerabilities, such as SQL injection and XSS. SQL injection attacks occur when an attacker injects malicious SQL code into a query, allowing them to interact with the backend database in unintended ways. Similarly, XSS attacks involve injecting malicious scripts into web pages, allowing attackers to steal sensitive information or hijack user sessions. WAFs can identify and block these types of attacks by recognizing malicious patterns in HTTP requests, such as suspicious SQL syntax or JavaScript code embedded in URLs or form fields. By filtering out these requests before they reach the application, WAFs help prevent attackers from exploiting these vulnerabilities.

WAFs also offer protection against a wide range of other web application attacks, including CSRF, remote file inclusion (RFI), and denial-of-service (DoS) attacks. CSRF attacks occur when an attacker tricks a user into performing unintended actions on a web application, often by embedding malicious links in emails or websites. WAFs can detect and block CSRF attempts by inspecting the origin and context of requests to ensure they are legitimate. RFI attacks involve exploiting vulnerabilities in the web application to include and execute remote files, often leading to server compromise. WAFs can prevent these attacks by identifying unusual file inclusion patterns and blocking them. Additionally, WAFs can help mitigate DoS attacks by limiting the rate of requests or identifying unusual traffic patterns indicative of an ongoing attack.

In addition to protecting against known attack vectors, WAFs also provide proactive security features, such as traffic monitoring and logging. By continuously monitoring web traffic, a WAF can detect and alert administrators to suspicious or anomalous activity. This provides valuable insights into the security posture of the web application and allows organizations to take immediate action if an attack is detected. WAFs can also log detailed information about blocked traffic, including the source of the attack, the type of attack attempted, and the URL or request that was targeted. These logs are valuable for forensic analysis and can help security teams identify attack trends, learn from past incidents, and improve overall security practices.

One of the critical aspects of implementing a WAF is configuring it correctly to ensure optimal protection without disrupting legitimate traffic. A WAF must be carefully tuned to differentiate between legitimate user requests and attack attempts. If the WAF is too aggressive in blocking traffic, it may mistakenly block legitimate users or interfere with the functionality of the web application. Conversely, if the WAF is too permissive, it may fail to block malicious requests, leaving the application vulnerable. Many WAFs offer a learning mode or a staging mode, where the firewall can observe traffic and generate security policies based on the patterns it observes. This allows administrators to fine-tune the configuration and ensure that the WAF is properly aligned with the needs of the web application while maintaining a high level of security.

Another consideration when implementing a WAF is the deployment model. WAFs can be deployed in various configurations, including as a cloud-based service, an on-premises appliance, or as a hybrid solution that combines the benefits of both. Cloud-based WAF services, such as those provided by AWS, Azure, or Cloudflare, are often easier to deploy and scale, as they are managed by third-party vendors and require less infrastructure management. These solutions are particularly well-suited for organizations that rely heavily on cloud-based infrastructure and want to offload the responsibility of managing a WAF. On-premises WAF appliances, on the other hand, provide more control over the security infrastructure but require more effort to manage and scale. Hybrid solutions combine the flexibility and scalability of cloud-based WAFs with the control of on-premises systems, allowing organizations to balance security and performance needs.

Once a WAF is deployed, it is essential to regularly update and maintain it to ensure that it provides ongoing protection against new and evolving threats. Attack techniques are constantly evolving, and a WAF that is not updated regularly may fail to detect new vulnerabilities or attack patterns. Many WAFs offer automatic updates to signature databases or provide access to threat intelligence feeds that allow the firewall to stay current with emerging threats. Additionally, regular testing and vulnerability scanning should be performed to identify potential gaps in the WAF configuration or areas where it may need adjustment. As new vulnerabilities and exploits are discovered, security teams must continually assess the WAF's effectiveness and make necessary updates to the rules and configurations.

It is also important to integrate a WAF with other security tools and processes to create a comprehensive security strategy. For example, a WAF should be part of a broader security monitoring and incident response framework, where it works in tandem with intrusion detection systems (IDS), security information and event management (SIEM) systems, and other network security tools. This integration allows for more effective threat detection and response, as WAFs can generate alerts and logs that can be analyzed alongside other security data. A holistic approach to web application security ensures that organizations can respond quickly to threats and maintain a strong defense posture across their entire infrastructure.

Web application firewalls are a critical component in securing modern web applications against a wide range of attacks. By filtering malicious traffic, enforcing secure coding practices, and providing real-time monitoring and alerts, WAFs offer valuable protection against threats like SQL injection, cross-site scripting, and denial-of-service attacks. When implemented correctly, WAFs significantly enhance the security of web applications while minimizing the risk of successful exploitation. Whether deployed as a cloud service, on-premises appliance, or hybrid solution, WAFs provide an essential layer of defense for organizations seeking to protect their web applications and ensure the availability, confidentiality, and integrity of their online services. Proper configuration, regular updates, and integration with other security tools are vital to ensuring that a WAF delivers its full potential in defending against the ever-evolving landscape of web application threats.

The Role of Network Segmentation in Server Hardening

Network segmentation is a critical strategy in modern cybersecurity, particularly when it comes to server hardening. As organizations increasingly rely on interconnected systems and complex infrastructures, the need to safeguard their servers from cyber threats has never been more important. Network segmentation involves dividing a larger network into smaller, isolated segments, or subnets, to reduce the attack surface and contain potential security breaches. This approach provides multiple layers of defense, making it more difficult for attackers to move laterally within a network after compromising a single server or device. By implementing network segmentation, organizations can bolster their server security and better control the flow of data, reducing the risk of widespread damage in the event of a security breach.

One of the key advantages of network segmentation is the ability to limit access to critical servers by isolating them from less secure parts of the network. Servers often house sensitive data, such as customer information, intellectual property, and financial records. By placing these servers within a dedicated, secured segment, organizations can enforce stricter access controls and reduce the chances of unauthorized access. For instance, a company's internal file server, which holds sensitive corporate documents, can be placed in a segmented network zone that is only accessible by authorized employees. Similarly, the database server that stores customer data can be isolated from general user traffic and protected by additional security measures, such as firewalls and intrusion detection systems.

With network segmentation, organizations can also implement the principle of least privilege more effectively. By segmenting the network, administrators can define granular access policies that specify who or what can access specific servers or resources. This means that even if an attacker compromises a server in one segment, they will face multiple hurdles before they can access more sensitive parts of the network. For example, an attacker who gains access to a server in a less-secure segment may be unable to reach critical infrastructure, such as a database or application server, without first bypassing additional security measures in place in other segments. This containment strategy is particularly important in environments where servers perform different roles and store different types of data, such as production, development, and testing environments.

In addition to providing security through isolation, network segmentation also helps to mitigate the risks associated with lateral movement within the network. Attackers often rely on lateral movement, a technique that involves moving from one compromised system to another, in order to escalate privileges and gain deeper access to the network. Once an attacker gains access to a low-level server, they may try to exploit vulnerabilities in other systems to achieve their goals. By implementing segmentation, organizations make it significantly harder for attackers to move freely across the network. Even if a hacker successfully compromises a device or server, the segmentation confines them to a limited area, and additional security measures—such as firewalls, access control lists (ACLs), and intrusion detection systems—can be applied to monitor and restrict the movement of unauthorized traffic between segments.

Network segmentation also plays a pivotal role in improving the performance and efficiency of security monitoring and incident response. By isolating sensitive data and critical servers into separate network segments, organizations can apply more focused and specialized monitoring techniques. For example, network traffic flowing between a production environment and a customer-facing web application may require more stringent monitoring and alerting compared to traffic flowing between employee workstations. By monitoring specific segments with tailored security tools, administrators can quickly detect unusual activity and take appropriate action to mitigate potential threats. This targeted approach not only reduces the noise in security alerts but also enhances the ability to detect sophisticated attacks, such as data exfiltration or advanced persistent threats (APTs), which often operate under the radar for extended periods of time.

One of the key elements of network segmentation is the use of firewalls and other access control mechanisms to restrict traffic between segments. Firewalls can be configured to enforce strict security policies, allowing only legitimate traffic to pass between network segments while blocking unauthorized or suspicious activity. For instance, a firewall can be set up to block access from the internet to an internal database server, ensuring that only authenticated users and authorized applications can communicate with it. In addition, segmentation allows for the use of virtual LANs (VLANs), which create logical divisions within a physical network to separate different types of traffic. This further enhances the security posture of an organization by enabling administrators to enforce stricter rules for each segment based on the sensitivity of the data and systems involved.

Another benefit of network segmentation in server hardening is the ability to isolate high-risk services and applications. Servers that run services such as email, web applications, and databases are often targeted by attackers due to their central role in business operations. By placing these services in separate, segmented parts of the network, organizations can isolate them from general user traffic and minimize their exposure to potential threats. For example, a public-facing web server that hosts the company's website can be isolated from the internal systems and applications used by employees. By doing so, the organization can ensure that even if the web server is compromised, the attacker cannot easily pivot to internal resources and systems that are more critical to the business.

Furthermore, network segmentation can support compliance with industry regulations and standards. Many industries, such as healthcare, finance, and government, require organizations to implement specific security measures to protect sensitive data. By segmenting networks, organizations can more easily enforce compliance with these requirements. For example, the Payment Card Industry Data Security Standard (PCI DSS) mandates that organizations protect cardholder data and maintain a secure network.

One of the requirements is to segment networks to isolate cardholder data from other parts of the network, making it easier to apply appropriate security controls, such as encryption and access controls, to protect the data. Network segmentation ensures that organizations meet the necessary compliance standards while reducing the risk of regulatory violations.

The process of network segmentation also aligns with a defense-in-depth approach to security. By applying multiple layers of protection, organizations can create a more resilient and robust network infrastructure. In addition to segmenting the network, organizations can implement other security measures, such as encryption, strong authentication mechanisms, and vulnerability management practices, to further harden the environment. Network segmentation complements these measures by reducing the potential impact of a single security failure. For example, if one segment is compromised due to a vulnerability, the segmented nature of the network ensures that the attacker cannot easily access other segments that may hold more critical data or systems.

To implement network segmentation successfully, organizations must first assess their network architecture and determine which resources and data need to be isolated. This assessment involves identifying sensitive systems, high-value assets, and critical infrastructure, and ensuring that these are placed in appropriately secured segments. Once the segments are established, access control policies should be defined, and firewalls and other security devices should be configured to enforce these policies. Ongoing monitoring and testing of the segmented network are essential to ensure that the segmentation is effective and that security gaps are addressed promptly.

Network segmentation plays a pivotal role in the overall hardening of server environments. By isolating sensitive servers, limiting lateral movement, and enabling focused security measures, segmentation enhances the security of the entire network infrastructure. As cyber threats continue to evolve, the need for comprehensive and proactive security strategies, such as network segmentation, has never been more important. By properly segmenting the network and applying appropriate security measures, organizations can significantly reduce the attack surface, contain potential breaches, and protect their critical server resources from malicious actors.

Securing Server Logs: Ensuring Integrity and Confidentiality

Server logs are essential for maintaining the security, health, and performance of a system. They record crucial information about the operation of a server, including user activity, system errors, application behavior, and security events. This information is invaluable for troubleshooting, monitoring, and auditing purposes. However, because logs contain sensitive data about the system's inner workings and potentially user actions, they can be a prime target for attackers. If compromised, server logs can be manipulated to cover tracks, mislead forensic investigations, or expose sensitive information. Therefore, securing server logs is a critical aspect of maintaining both the integrity and confidentiality of a system. Ensuring that logs are properly protected from tampering and unauthorized access is fundamental to supporting incident response, compliance requirements, and ongoing security efforts.

The first step in securing server logs is to ensure their integrity. The integrity of a log file refers to the assurance that the data within the log has not been altered or tampered with, either maliciously or accidentally. Once a log entry is written, it is crucial that it remains unchanged to provide accurate, trustworthy records for future analysis. If an attacker gains access to the server, they may attempt to modify or delete log files to cover their tracks, making it difficult for administrators to detect and respond to the attack. To prevent this, logs should be stored in a location where only authorized users and processes can access them, and the files should be protected by appropriate file permissions. In many systems, administrators can configure logs to be immutable, meaning that once data is written, it cannot be altered or deleted unless authorized by a specific process.

One effective method for securing the integrity of server logs is by implementing cryptographic techniques such as hashing and digital signatures. A hash function can be applied to log files to create a unique fingerprint of the data. This fingerprint can then be stored securely, allowing the administrator to compare it with the current state of the log files to verify that they have not been tampered with. If the log file is altered in any way, the hash value will change, signaling potential manipulation. In addition, digital signatures can be used to verify both the integrity and authenticity of log entries. By signing each log entry with a private key, organizations can ensure that the logs have not been modified and that they originate from a trusted source. These cryptographic methods are particularly valuable for maintaining the integrity of logs in environments where logs are stored off-site or remotely.

Another critical aspect of log security is ensuring their confidentiality. Logs may contain sensitive information, such as IP addresses, usernames, system details, or even the content of communications between users and the server. If logs are exposed to unauthorized individuals, this information can be misused. Attackers who gain access to server logs could identify vulnerabilities or weaknesses in the system, launch additional attacks, or collect personally identifiable information for use in further exploits. To prevent this, server logs should be encrypted both at rest and in transit. Encryption ensures that even if an attacker gains access to the log files, they cannot read or exploit the information contained within them without the appropriate decryption keys. For logs that need to be transmitted across a network, secure communication protocols such as TLS should be used to prevent interception and ensure that the logs remain confidential during transit.

Access controls are essential to safeguarding log data from unauthorized users. Server logs should be restricted to specific personnel who have a legitimate need to access them, such as system administrators or security teams. Access to logs should be based on the principle of least privilege, ensuring that users and applications have only the minimum level of access necessary to perform their tasks. This means that even if an attacker compromises a user account with excessive privileges, they will not be able to access sensitive logs unless authorized. Role-based access control (RBAC) is a useful framework for managing permissions and ensuring that access to logs is granted based on the user's role within the organization. Additionally, logs themselves should be monitored for unauthorized access attempts, and alerts should be triggered if abnormal or suspicious access patterns are detected. Logging access to log files provides an additional layer of auditability, ensuring that any attempt to access logs is recorded and can be investigated if needed.

In addition to securing logs from unauthorized access, organizations must also ensure that logs are retained and managed according to organizational and regulatory requirements. Many industries are subject to data retention regulations that specify how long logs must be stored, and under what conditions they must be kept secure. For example, in the financial industry, logs related to transactions may need to be stored for several years to comply with regulatory standards. A well-defined log retention policy helps organizations manage the lifecycle of logs and ensures that logs are preserved for the required duration while minimizing unnecessary exposure. The policy should also dictate how logs are archived and destroyed once they are no longer needed, ensuring that old logs are securely deleted to prevent unauthorized access or data leaks.

Automating the process of log management is another way to ensure that logs are properly secured. Log aggregation tools can be used to collect logs from various servers, applications, and network devices and store them in a centralized location for easier analysis and management. These tools can also be configured to apply security measures, such as encryption, compression, and hashing, automatically as logs are generated. Centralized logging allows for more efficient monitoring and analysis, as it provides a single point of access for security teams to review logs from across the infrastructure. Additionally, automated systems can flag anomalies in log data, such as failed login attempts or unusual network activity, helping security teams identify potential threats in real time. Integrating these tools with a security information and event management (SIEM) system enhances the organization's ability to detect and respond to incidents quickly.

Another critical consideration for securing server logs is ensuring that log files are adequately backed up. Logs are a valuable source of evidence for forensic investigations and incident response, and losing this data can severely hinder efforts to understand and resolve security incidents. Backups of log data should be stored securely, preferably in a separate location from the main server infrastructure, to protect them from being destroyed or altered in the event of a breach. Regular backups should be part of the organization's disaster recovery and business continuity plans, ensuring that log data is available when needed and can be restored in case of hardware failure or data loss.

Finally, organizations must continuously assess and audit their log security practices. Security is not a one-time effort, and as threats evolve, so too must the strategies used to secure server logs. Regular security assessments, penetration tests, and audits can help identify vulnerabilities in log management processes and uncover areas for improvement. Logs themselves should be reviewed periodically to ensure they are being generated, stored, and protected according to the organization's security policies and regulatory requirements. By maintaining an ongoing process of review and improvement, organizations can adapt to emerging threats and maintain a strong security posture.

Securing server logs is a multifaceted task that requires a combination of technical measures, policies, and ongoing management. Ensuring the integrity and confidentiality of logs is essential to maintaining a secure environment and providing a reliable record of system activity. From implementing encryption and access controls to regular monitoring and auditing, securing server logs is a critical component of any comprehensive server hardening strategy. With the right measures in place, organizations can safeguard their logs, protect sensitive data, and ensure that their servers remain secure in the face of evolving cyber threats.

Using Security-Enhanced Tools for File Integrity Monitoring

File integrity monitoring (FIM) is a crucial component of a comprehensive security strategy designed to detect unauthorized changes to files and directories on a system. The integrity of files, especially system and configuration files, is a key indicator of the health and security of an IT environment. If an attacker compromises a system, they often attempt to alter files to maintain persistence, escalate privileges, or disable security mechanisms. Using security-enhanced tools for file integrity monitoring provides a proactive approach to detect and respond to unauthorized changes in real time, ensuring that the system remains secure and compliant with regulatory standards.

File integrity monitoring tools are designed to monitor files for changes, including modifications, deletions, and creations. These tools compare the current state of files with a baseline or reference snapshot, which contains known-good configurations and file attributes. Any deviation from the established baseline can indicate a potential security incident, such as a system compromise or malware infection. Security-enhanced FIM tools go beyond basic file monitoring by integrating advanced techniques, such as cryptographic hashing, real-time alerts, and integration with other security mechanisms, to provide a more robust defense against file tampering and unauthorized access.

One of the most powerful techniques employed by security-enhanced FIM tools is cryptographic hashing. When a file is created or modified, the tool generates a unique cryptographic hash, such as SHA-256, based on the file's content. This hash serves as a digital fingerprint of the file. At regular intervals, the FIM tool recalculates the hash and compares it to the previously stored value. If the hashes match, it indicates that the file has not been altered. However, if the hashes do not match, it signifies that the file's contents have changed. This technique ensures that even subtle changes to file contents—such as those made by a malicious actor to introduce a backdoor—can be detected. By using cryptographic hashes, FIM tools provide a high level of accuracy and reliability, ensuring that the integrity of critical files is maintained.

The real-time monitoring feature of security-enhanced FIM tools is another essential aspect of their functionality. Detecting changes after they occur is useful, but it is even more critical to identify and respond to suspicious activity as it happens. Real-time alerts enable security teams to take immediate action when an unauthorized change is detected. For example, if a configuration file is unexpectedly altered or a sensitive document is deleted, the FIM tool can trigger an alert to notify administrators of the anomaly. These alerts can be configured to be as granular as necessary, ensuring that only relevant events are flagged while avoiding unnecessary noise. With real-time monitoring, organizations can respond quickly to security threats, reducing the time an attacker has to exploit the system and minimizing the potential damage caused.

Moreover, security-enhanced FIM tools are often designed to work in conjunction with other security measures, such as intrusion detection systems (IDS), security information and event management (SIEM) platforms, and endpoint protection solutions. By integrating FIM tools with these systems, organizations can create a more cohesive and effective security posture. For instance, file integrity alerts generated by the FIM tool can be fed into a SIEM system, where they are correlated with other events and analyzed for potential threats. If the system detects a pattern of suspicious activity, such as multiple failed login attempts followed by unauthorized file modifications, it can trigger an automated response, such as isolating the affected system or blocking the malicious user. This integration enhances the overall security response and ensures that no single layer of protection is operating in isolation.

File integrity monitoring tools can also be configured to monitor a wide range of files and directories, including operating system files, application files, configuration files, and logs. Monitoring system files, in particular, is critical, as they often contain sensitive information about system configurations, user accounts, and network settings. Attackers frequently target these files to escalate their privileges, disable security features, or cover their tracks after compromising a system. By monitoring these files for unauthorized changes, organizations can detect attempts to manipulate critical system configurations before they lead to significant security breaches. Application files, too, should be closely monitored, as attackers may seek to alter application code or configuration files to insert malicious functionality or to disable logging and security features.

In addition to monitoring file integrity, security-enhanced FIM tools provide mechanisms for auditing changes to ensure compliance with industry regulations and internal security policies. Many regulatory frameworks, such as the Payment Card Industry Data Security

Standard (PCI DSS), the Health Insurance Portability and Accountability Act (HIPAA), and the General Data Protection Regulation (GDPR), require organizations to maintain detailed logs of system activity, including changes to critical files. Security-enhanced FIM tools can automatically generate audit trails that document changes to files, including who made the change, when it occurred, and what was modified. These logs are valuable for demonstrating compliance during audits and for investigating security incidents. In addition, the ability to generate forensic reports from the FIM system can provide security teams with valuable insights into the timeline of a breach or compromise, helping them understand how the attack unfolded and what actions need to be taken to prevent future incidents.

For organizations that rely on cloud-based infrastructure, securing file integrity in a distributed environment presents unique challenges. Many cloud environments involve shared resources and dynamic configurations that make traditional file integrity monitoring more complex. Security-enhanced FIM tools designed for cloud environments can help address these challenges by extending monitoring capabilities to cloud instances, containers, and virtual machines. These tools can monitor file integrity across multiple cloud providers and across hybrid cloud environments, ensuring that security policies are applied consistently and that no unauthorized changes are made to cloud-based resources. By implementing FIM in the cloud, organizations can maintain the same level of protection as they would with on-premises systems, ensuring that sensitive data and applications hosted in the cloud remain secure.

One of the most effective ways to implement security-enhanced file integrity monitoring is through the use of open-source and commercial tools tailored to specific system environments. Open-source FIM solutions provide flexibility and customization, allowing organizations to modify and extend the tool to meet their unique needs. Commercial tools, on the other hand, typically offer more robust features, dedicated support, and integration with other enterprise security systems. Some commercial tools come with advanced features, such as machine learning-based anomaly detection, which can identify unusual patterns of file access or modification that may indicate an advanced attack. The choice between open-source and commercial FIM solutions depends on the organization's size, budget, and specific security needs.

In environments where file integrity is crucial for maintaining trust and operational security, using security-enhanced tools for monitoring file changes is indispensable. These tools provide organizations with the capability to detect unauthorized alterations in real time, improve incident response efforts, and ensure compliance with industry standards. By combining cryptographic integrity checks, real-time monitoring, integration with other security systems, and comprehensive auditing, security-enhanced file integrity monitoring tools can significantly enhance an organization's ability to detect and prevent attacks that target critical files and applications. Whether implemented on-premises or in the cloud, these tools provide a robust and proactive defense against threats to system integrity.

Preventing Buffer Overflow Attacks on Servers

Buffer overflow attacks have long been a major concern in the world of cybersecurity. These attacks occur when a program writes more data to a buffer than it is allocated to store, which can cause data to overwrite adjacent memory locations. This results in unpredictable behavior, which attackers can exploit to gain control over the system. When it comes to servers, the consequences of a buffer overflow attack can be particularly devastating, as it can lead to full system compromise, unauthorized access, and the execution of arbitrary code. Preventing buffer overflow attacks is therefore crucial for maintaining the security and integrity of servers, especially given the increasing sophistication of cyber threats.

A buffer is a temporary data storage area, often used to hold data during input or output operations. In many applications, especially in low-level programming languages like C and C++, buffers are created with a fixed size. If a program does not properly check the amount of data being written to a buffer, it can inadvertently allow data to overflow into adjacent memory locations, potentially leading to a range of issues. In a buffer overflow attack, the attacker takes advantage of this flaw by providing input that exceeds the buffer's capacity, causing the program to overwrite critical memory structures. By doing so, the attacker can gain control over the execution flow of the program and potentially execute arbitrary code on the server.

The first step in preventing buffer overflow attacks is to adopt secure coding practices. Secure coding ensures that applications are designed with security in mind from the outset. One of the key principles in secure coding is to always check the size of data before it is written to a buffer. This can be done by validating user input, ensuring that it fits within the buffer's limits, and rejecting any input that exceeds these boundaries. Additionally, programming languages such as C and C++ offer functions that allow developers to specify the maximum amount of data that can be written to a buffer, helping to mitigate the risk of buffer overflows. Developers should use these safer functions, such as snprintf() instead of sprintf(), to avoid vulnerabilities in string manipulation.

Another important technique for preventing buffer overflow attacks is implementing bounds checking. Bounds checking involves verifying that the size of input data does not exceed the allocated buffer size. Many modern programming languages and frameworks, including Java and Python, inherently perform bounds checking, making them less vulnerable to buffer overflow attacks compared to low-level languages like C. However, even in languages that automatically perform bounds checking, developers must remain vigilant and avoid practices that could lead to other types of vulnerabilities. For instance, handling user input properly and sanitizing it before processing can prevent attackers from exploiting potential weaknesses in the application.

In addition to secure coding practices, compilers can be configured to help prevent buffer overflow attacks. Many modern compilers have built-in security features that can help detect and prevent buffer overflows at the compilation stage. For example, the Stack Canaries technique is a defense mechanism that places a small value (the canary) just before the return address in the program's stack. If the buffer overflow overwrites the canary, the program detects the modification and halts before any harm can be done. Additionally, many compilers support the use of Data Execution Prevention (DEP) and Address Space Layout Randomization (ASLR), both of which make it more difficult for attackers to predict the location of critical memory regions and inject malicious code into the system.

Stack protection is another technique commonly used to safeguard servers against buffer overflow attacks. Stack protection mechanisms, such as ProPolice or GCC's -fstack-protector flag, can help prevent attackers from exploiting buffer overflows by detecting changes to the stack during runtime. These protections add a layer of security to the program by placing additional checks to ensure that the return address is not altered by a buffer overflow. When the stack protection detects an anomaly, it can terminate the process immediately, preventing the overflow from affecting the server's memory and blocking the potential for code execution.

While secure coding and compiler-level protections can help mitigate buffer overflow vulnerabilities, they are not foolproof. Therefore, it is crucial to employ additional layers of defense, such as using modern operating systems that have built-in security features designed to thwart buffer overflow attacks. For example, modern operating systems often implement Data Execution Prevention (DEP), which prevents execution from certain areas of memory, such as the stack, where attackers typically inject malicious code. DEP works by marking sections of memory as non-executable, meaning that even if an attacker manages to inject code into these areas, it cannot be executed.

Similarly, Address Space Layout Randomization (ASLR) is a technique employed by modern operating systems to randomize the memory addresses used by system and application processes. By randomizing the memory layout, ASLR makes it more difficult for an attacker to predict where specific functions or buffers are located, making it harder for them to exploit a buffer overflow vulnerability. With ASLR in place, even if an attacker can execute malicious code, they will likely be unable to determine the correct memory location to target.

To further protect against buffer overflow attacks, organizations should implement proper server configuration and access controls. For example, reducing the attack surface by disabling unnecessary services and limiting the number of open ports can help mitigate the impact of a potential attack. A principle of least privilege should be applied, ensuring that users and processes are given the minimum level of access necessary to perform their functions. This reduces the likelihood that an attacker will be able to exploit a buffer overflow to gain access to critical system functions or sensitive data.

In addition, regularly updating software and applying security patches is essential for reducing the risk of buffer overflow attacks. Many buffer overflow vulnerabilities are discovered and patched by software vendors over time. By ensuring that all applications and server software are up to date with the latest patches and security fixes, organizations can reduce their exposure to known buffer overflow vulnerabilities. Automated patch management systems can help ensure that patches are applied promptly and consistently across the organization's servers, preventing attackers from exploiting outdated or unpatched software.

Organizations should also consider using intrusion detection and prevention systems (IDPS) to monitor for signs of buffer overflow attacks. These systems can detect unusual patterns of behavior, such as an unexpected surge in traffic or attempts to access restricted areas of the server, and alert administrators to potential attacks. By combining proactive monitoring with other security measures, such as firewalls and antivirus software, organizations can improve their ability to detect and respond to buffer overflow attacks in real time.

In summary, preventing buffer overflow attacks on servers requires a multi-layered approach that combines secure coding practices, compiler protections, operating system security features, and proper server configuration. By following these strategies, organizations can significantly reduce the risk of buffer overflow vulnerabilities and protect their systems from potential exploits. Regular software updates, patch management, and monitoring further strengthen the defense against these types of attacks, ensuring that servers remain secure and resilient in the face of evolving cyber threats.

Implementing Rate Limiting to Prevent Abuse

Rate limiting is a powerful technique used to control the amount of traffic or requests that a server or an application can handle over a specific period of time. It is particularly useful in mitigating various forms of abuse, including denial of service (DoS) attacks, brute-force login attempts, and overloading resources with excessive requests. As the number of users and applications interacting with services grows, ensuring that these services remain available and secure is critical. Rate limiting plays an essential role in maintaining this balance by allowing legitimate users to access resources while preventing malicious users or automated bots from overwhelming the system with high volumes of requests.

The primary goal of rate limiting is to restrict the number of requests a client can make to a server or API within a defined time window. This is especially important in protecting services that are exposed to the internet, such as login pages, APIs, and web applications, where high traffic volumes can quickly lead to system degradation or downtime. Without rate limiting in place, attackers can flood a service with requests, attempting to exhaust system resources or exploit weaknesses, such as login forms, to gain unauthorized access. In addition, excessive requests can also be a form of resource abuse, where legitimate users are denied service because the server is too busy handling malicious requests.

To implement rate limiting effectively, it is crucial to identify which parts of the application are most susceptible to abuse and to define the appropriate rate limits for each. For example, login endpoints are common targets for brute-force attacks, where attackers use automated tools to try a large number of username and password combinations in a short period. By limiting the number of login attempts allowed within a certain time frame, organizations can prevent attackers from successfully guessing credentials. Similarly, APIs exposed to external users may be targeted by bots or malicious users who attempt to overwhelm the server by sending a large number of requests in a short time. Rate limiting on these endpoints ensures that only legitimate users can access the service and helps protect against API abuse.

There are several techniques for implementing rate limiting, each with its strengths and use cases. One common method is the token bucket algorithm, which allows clients to make a burst of requests up to a defined limit but then requires them to wait before making further requests once their quota has been consumed. This approach provides some flexibility in allowing short bursts of traffic while still enforcing a maximum rate of requests over time. The leaky bucket algorithm is another popular approach, where requests are allowed to flow through at a fixed rate, and any excessive requests are queued or discarded, depending on the configuration. The leaky bucket algorithm is effective in preventing traffic spikes that might otherwise overwhelm a server.

Another widely used technique is fixed window rate limiting, where a defined period (e.g., one minute or one hour) is used to track the number of requests made by a client. If the client exceeds the allowed limit within the time window, additional requests are denied until the window resets. While simple to implement, this method can result in some unfairness if a client makes a large number of requests just before the window resets, leading to bursts of traffic that can still impact the server. Sliding window rate limiting solves this problem by continuously calculating the request count based on a rolling time window, ensuring that traffic spikes are more evenly distributed.

To effectively prevent abuse, rate limiting should be applied not only at the level of individual users but also across broader entities, such as IP addresses or API keys. This approach ensures that attackers cannot bypass rate limiting by changing their IP address or using multiple accounts. However, in some cases, applying rate limits at the IP level may be too coarse, as legitimate users sharing the same IP address, such as those in a corporate environment or behind a NAT (Network Address Translation) device, may be unfairly impacted. In such cases, organizations should consider implementing more granular rate limiting that accounts for factors like user-agent strings, session IDs, or other unique identifiers that help differentiate between users without overburdening the system with excessive rate limits.

While rate limiting is a powerful tool in preventing abuse, it is important to implement it in a way that does not interfere with the user experience. Rate limiting thresholds should be chosen carefully to ensure that legitimate users can access the service without excessive delay or disruption. For example, a reasonable number of login attempts or API calls per minute should be allowed to avoid frustrating users who may need to retry their requests for legitimate reasons. On the other hand, rate limits should be set low enough to prevent malicious users from overwhelming the server. This balance between security and usability is a key consideration when designing rate limiting rules, and testing is essential to determine the appropriate limits for different use cases.

One of the challenges in implementing rate limiting is managing distributed denial of service (DDoS) attacks, where attackers use a large number of compromised devices (botnets) to send massive volumes of traffic to a target. Traditional rate limiting methods may struggle to mitigate DDoS attacks effectively, as the attack traffic often originates from many different IP addresses. In such cases, organizations can enhance their rate limiting strategy by using advanced techniques like challenge-response tests (e.g., CAPTCHAs) or by integrating with external DDoS protection services, which can absorb and filter large-scale attacks before they reach the target server. These services typically use traffic analysis and machine learning models to distinguish between legitimate and malicious traffic, applying rate limiting dynamically to protect the server from overload.

Another important consideration when implementing rate limiting is the need to provide users with feedback when they hit the limit. Clear and informative error messages help users understand why their requests are being blocked and how long they need to wait before they can try again. Without proper feedback, users may be confused or frustrated by the restrictions, leading to a poor experience. Additionally, providing a mechanism for users to request higher limits, such as through a service desk or automatic escalation for trusted users, can help prevent rate limiting from becoming an obstacle to legitimate use cases.

Logging and monitoring are essential components of any rate limiting strategy. By keeping detailed logs of rate-limited requests, administrators can gain insights into traffic patterns and identify potential abuse. This can help fine-tune the rate limiting rules to strike the right balance between security and usability. Furthermore, real-time monitoring tools can provide immediate alerts when the rate limits are exceeded, allowing security teams to quickly respond to potential attacks. This proactive approach ensures that rate limiting is continuously optimized to defend against emerging threats without adversely impacting the user experience.

To summarize, implementing rate limiting is an essential practice for preventing abuse and ensuring the security and availability of server resources. By carefully selecting rate limiting strategies, applying limits based on unique identifiers, and balancing security with user experience, organizations can protect their servers from abuse, reduce the impact of DDoS attacks, and maintain a high level of service. Integrating rate limiting with other security measures, such as challenge-response tests and external DDoS mitigation services, further strengthens defenses and ensures that systems remain resilient in the face of growing cyber threats.

Securing APIs on Servers Against Common Vulnerabilities

Application Programming Interfaces (APIs) have become the backbone of modern software development, enabling different systems and applications to communicate with each other. APIs are widely used to expose server functionalities and allow data to flow seamlessly between platforms, applications, and services. However, due to their exposure to external clients and third-party integrations, APIs are often targeted by attackers. Securing APIs against common vulnerabilities is essential for maintaining the integrity and confidentiality of data, ensuring that malicious actors cannot exploit these interfaces to gain unauthorized access, manipulate data, or disrupt services. Given the critical role APIs play in today's interconnected environments, ensuring their security requires a multifaceted approach that addresses common vulnerabilities, enforces access controls, and continuously monitors for abnormal behavior.

One of the most common vulnerabilities in APIs is insufficient authentication and authorization mechanisms. APIs often handle sensitive data and provide access to backend systems, making them an attractive target for attackers seeking unauthorized access. Insecure authentication practices, such as relying solely on basic authentication or weak password management, can leave APIs exposed to brute-force attacks or credential stuffing. Similarly, weak or misconfigured authorization controls may allow unauthorized users to access resources they should not have permission to interact with. To address these vulnerabilities, organizations must implement strong authentication mechanisms, such as OAuth, OpenID Connect, or API keys, and enforce robust password policies. Additionally, strict access controls should be implemented to ensure that users can only access the resources they are authorized to use, based on their role or privileges. These mechanisms should be regularly tested and updated to prevent exploits based on outdated or easily bypassed authentication methods.

Another significant vulnerability is the lack of input validation, which can expose APIs to a wide range of attacks, including SQL injection, cross-site scripting (XSS), and other injection-based attacks. APIs often accept user input, and without proper validation, malicious data can be sent to the server, where it may be executed or stored improperly. For example, a simple SQL injection attack can allow attackers to manipulate queries, access sensitive data, or even delete records from a database. Similarly, XSS attacks can inject malicious scripts into the API response, potentially compromising the client-side application or stealing sensitive user information. To mitigate these risks, input validation should be performed rigorously on both incoming and outgoing data. All input should be validated for type, length, format, and range, and any potentially harmful characters should be sanitized or rejected. Using parameterized queries for database access and avoiding direct execution of user-supplied data are also key techniques to prevent injection attacks.

Another vulnerability frequently found in APIs is improper handling of sensitive data, such as personal information, financial records, or authentication tokens. APIs often deal with sensitive data, and if this data is not properly protected, it can be intercepted, manipulated, or exposed by attackers. One of the most important steps in securing APIs is ensuring that data is encrypted both in transit and at rest. APIs should use secure communication protocols, such as HTTPS with SSL/TLS encryption, to protect data during transmission. This ensures that even if the communication is intercepted, the data remains unreadable to attackers. Additionally, sensitive data stored on the server should be encrypted using strong encryption algorithms, and access to this data should be tightly controlled. Authentication tokens and session information should also be handled securely, with tokens being stored in secure locations and never exposed to unauthorized parties.

API rate limiting is another critical aspect of securing APIs against abuse. Without rate limiting, APIs are vulnerable to denial-of-service (DoS) attacks, where attackers flood the API with an overwhelming number of requests, rendering it unresponsive or consuming excessive system resources. Rate limiting helps to ensure that APIs can handle traffic in a controlled manner by limiting the number of requests that a client can make within a specified time period. By implementing rate limiting, organizations can prevent abuse and mitigate the impact of DDoS attacks. Additionally, rate limiting can be combined with other security measures, such as IP blocking or CAPTCHA challenges, to further enhance protection against malicious traffic.

Cross-origin resource sharing (CORS) misconfigurations are another common vulnerability that affects APIs. CORS is a mechanism that allows web applications running at one origin to make requests to a different origin, such as accessing an API from a different domain. While CORS is essential for enabling cross-origin requests, misconfigurations can expose APIs to attacks such as data theft, unauthorized access, or man-in-the-middle attacks. For example, if CORS is not properly configured, malicious websites could make unauthorized requests to an API, stealing sensitive data or manipulating resources. To prevent this, APIs should implement strict CORS policies, allowing only trusted origins to make requests. CORS headers should be configured to restrict access to specific domains and to limit the types of requests that are allowed.

Another important aspect of API security is ensuring that proper logging and monitoring are in place to detect and respond to security incidents. APIs are often targeted by attackers attempting to exploit vulnerabilities or perform unauthorized actions, and without proper monitoring, these attacks can go undetected. API logs should include detailed information about incoming requests, user actions, and any errors or unusual behavior that occurs during interaction with the API. This data can be invaluable for detecting security incidents, identifying trends in suspicious activity, and responding to potential threats. API logs should be stored securely and analyzed regularly for anomalies, and security teams should be notified promptly when unusual activity is detected. Additionally, organizations should implement an incident response plan that includes specific procedures for handling API security breaches, ensuring that security teams are prepared to take immediate action if an attack occurs.

One of the most effective ways to secure APIs is through regular security testing and vulnerability assessments. Penetration testing, in which ethical hackers attempt to exploit known vulnerabilities in the API, can help identify weaknesses that might be overlooked during the development process. Security testing tools, such as static application security testing (SAST) and dynamic application security testing (DAST), can be used to scan the API for vulnerabilities such as insecure authentication mechanisms, injection flaws, and weak encryption. Regular vulnerability assessments help organizations stay ahead of emerging threats and ensure that their APIs are up to date with the latest security patches and best practices.

API security is an ongoing process that requires continuous attention and improvement. As the threat landscape evolves and attackers develop new techniques, organizations must stay vigilant and adapt their security measures to address new risks. This includes keeping up with the latest security standards and industry best practices, regularly reviewing API access logs, and staying informed about emerging vulnerabilities. By following a proactive, defense-in-depth approach to API security, organizations can reduce the risk of data breaches, unauthorized access, and other security incidents that could compromise the integrity of their systems and the safety of their users.

Securing APIs on servers requires a multifaceted approach that includes strong authentication mechanisms, input validation, data encryption, rate limiting, and regular testing. By addressing common vulnerabilities, implementing best practices, and continuously monitoring and updating security measures, organizations can ensure that their APIs remain secure and resilient to attacks. As APIs continue to play a critical role in modern application ecosystems, protecting them from abuse and exploitation must be a top priority for any organization concerned with maintaining the security and privacy of its data.

Preventing Cross-Site Scripting (XSS) on Web Servers

Cross-Site Scripting (XSS) attacks are among the most prevalent and dangerous types of vulnerabilities that web servers face today. XSS attacks occur when an attacker is able to inject malicious scripts into web pages viewed by other users. These scripts are often executed by the victim's browser, which can lead to various harmful consequences such as the theft of sensitive data, session hijacking, and redirection to malicious websites. Given the widespread use of web applications and the reliance on user-generated content, protecting against XSS attacks is crucial for the security and integrity of web servers. Implementing measures to prevent XSS requires a multi-layered approach, combining secure coding practices, input sanitization, output encoding, and continuous monitoring.

At its core, XSS exploits a weakness in the way web applications handle untrusted data. Web applications often interact with user-generated content, such as form inputs, search queries, and URLs, which can be manipulated to include malicious scripts. When this untrusted data is incorporated into web pages without proper validation or sanitization, attackers can inject malicious JavaScript code that is then executed by the browser of unsuspecting users. This can lead to a range of malicious activities, including stealing cookies, capturing keystrokes, defacing websites, or redirecting users to phishing sites. To mitigate these risks, it is essential to ensure that web applications correctly handle and validate all incoming data before it is used to dynamically generate web pages.

The first step in preventing XSS attacks is to sanitize and validate all user input. This involves ensuring that user inputs are properly filtered for any potentially harmful content, such as script tags or event handlers. Many web frameworks provide built-in functions for input validation, which can help ensure that the data adheres to expected formats. For example, if an application expects a user's email address, the input should be validated to ensure that it conforms to the correct email format and does not contain any script elements. Input sanitization can also involve removing or escaping any special characters that could be interpreted as code by the web browser. This step is crucial in reducing the chances of malicious code being injected into the application.

While input sanitization is important, it is not enough on its own to prevent XSS. Output encoding is another critical defense mechanism that ensures that any data returned to the browser is properly encoded before being rendered on the page. Output encoding ensures that user-supplied data is treated as plain text rather than executable code. For instance, characters such as <, >, and &, which are commonly used in HTML and JavaScript, should be encoded as their respective HTML entities (<, >, and &). This prevents the browser from interpreting the input as HTML or JavaScript, thus mitigating the risk of an XSS attack. Output encoding should be applied wherever user-generated content is displayed, including form inputs, search results, and URL parameters.

To further protect against XSS, web servers should implement proper content security policies (CSPs). A CSP is a security measure that restricts the sources from which content can be loaded on a web page, including scripts, images, and styles. By defining a strict CSP, web servers can block the execution of malicious scripts from unauthorized sources. For example, CSP can prevent inline JavaScript from executing or disallow scripts from external domains that are not explicitly trusted. Implementing a strong CSP is a key defense mechanism in preventing XSS attacks because it limits the scope of what attackers can achieve, even if they manage to inject malicious code into a page.

Another important measure to prevent XSS is the use of HTTP-only and secure flags for cookies. These flags are critical for ensuring that cookies containing sensitive information, such as session identifiers, are not accessible via client-side JavaScript. By marking cookies as HTTP-only, they become inaccessible to scripts running in the browser, thereby preventing attackers from stealing session cookies via XSS. The secure flag ensures that cookies are only sent over HTTPS connections, adding an extra layer of protection to prevent interception by attackers on unsecured networks.

Cross-Site Scripting can also be mitigated by adopting a secure coding philosophy, where developers are aware of and follow best practices to reduce the risk of introducing vulnerabilities. One of the most common practices for defending against XSS is to avoid mixing code and data in the web application. This can be achieved by using secure templating engines that automatically escape data when embedding it into HTML. These engines ensure that user input is treated as data, not executable code, and automatically apply output encoding to prevent XSS vulnerabilities. Using modern web development frameworks that promote secure coding practices, such as Angular, React, or Django, can also provide additional built-in protections against XSS by handling input sanitization and output encoding automatically.

Educating developers about the risks and mitigation strategies for XSS is another critical step in preventing attacks. While some basic XSS prevention techniques are well-documented, the variety of possible attack vectors makes it essential for developers to stay informed about the latest best practices and security guidelines. Regular code reviews and security audits should be conducted to identify potential XSS vulnerabilities before they are deployed into production environments. Automated security testing tools, such as static application security testing (SAST) and dynamic application security testing (DAST) tools, can also be used to scan for vulnerabilities in the codebase, flagging potential XSS flaws that need to be addressed.

Web servers should also adopt a policy of strict security updates and patching to ensure that known vulnerabilities are addressed promptly. XSS vulnerabilities are frequently discovered in both web applications and web server software, and attackers often target unpatched systems. By regularly updating the server software, web application frameworks, and libraries used in the application, organizations can minimize the risk of known vulnerabilities being exploited by attackers. Using tools like package managers and version control systems helps ensure that dependencies are up to date and that security patches are applied without delay.

Finally, implementing proper logging and monitoring is essential for detecting and responding to XSS attacks. Logs should be configured to capture relevant information about user input and the execution of scripts on the server. Monitoring systems can be set up to alert administrators when unusual activity is detected, such as a sudden spike in invalid input or a high number of requests to sensitive endpoints. This early detection capability allows security teams to respond quickly and mitigate the impact of an attack before it can cause significant damage.

In summary, preventing Cross-Site Scripting attacks on web servers requires a multi-layered approach that includes secure coding practices, input validation, output encoding, and robust security measures like CSP and secure cookie handling. By implementing these defenses, organizations can significantly reduce the likelihood of XSS vulnerabilities being exploited, ensuring the safety and integrity of their web applications. The combination of proactive security measures, continuous monitoring, and regular updates is essential for protecting against the evolving threat landscape associated with XSS attacks.

Using Security Information and Event Management (SIEM) Systems

In today's cybersecurity landscape, organizations face an ever-growing number of security threats, ranging from sophisticated cyberattacks to simple configuration errors that can compromise sensitive data. To detect, analyze, and respond to these threats effectively, many organizations turn to Security Information and Event Management (SIEM) systems. A SIEM system plays a crucial role in centralizing the collection, normalization, and analysis of security-related data from a wide variety of sources within an organization's infrastructure. By providing real-time monitoring, advanced analytics, and incident response capabilities, SIEM systems enable organizations to identify potential security breaches, understand the context of threats, and take proactive steps to protect their networks and data.

At its core, a SIEM system collects log data from various sources such as firewalls, intrusion detection systems (IDS), servers, operating systems, applications, and network devices. These logs provide a detailed account of events occurring within an organization's IT environment, such as user logins, file access, system changes, and network traffic. However, raw log data is often voluminous and difficult to interpret on its own, making it challenging for security teams to detect suspicious activity or potential attacks. This is where a SIEM system comes into play, offering a centralized platform to aggregate, normalize, and analyze security events in real time. By processing and correlating logs from multiple sources, SIEM systems help security analysts identify patterns of behavior that may indicate a security incident.

One of the most valuable features of a SIEM system is its ability to provide real-time monitoring and alerting. By continuously collecting and analyzing log data, SIEM systems can detect anomalies and trigger alerts when certain predefined conditions or thresholds are met. For example, if an unusually high number of failed login attempts are detected from a single IP address, the SIEM system can immediately generate an alert, prompting security personnel to investigate further. Similarly, if there is a sudden spike in network traffic from a particular server or device, the SIEM system can flag this as a potential denial-of-service (DoS) attack or data exfiltration attempt. The ability to detect these issues in real time is crucial for minimizing the impact of a security breach and responding to threats before they escalate.

SIEM systems rely heavily on event correlation to identify complex attack patterns and security incidents. Event correlation involves analyzing the relationships between different events and data points across the network to identify suspicious activity that may not be immediately apparent from individual logs. For example, a SIEM system may correlate a series of failed login attempts with the subsequent successful login from the same IP address, followed by the execution of administrative commands. This sequence of events could indicate a brute-force attack followed by unauthorized access to sensitive data. By correlating multiple events in this way, SIEM systems can help security teams identify and respond to sophisticated attacks that may involve multiple stages or tactics.

Another important capability of SIEM systems is incident detection and response. Once a potential security threat is identified, the SIEM system provides security teams with detailed information about the incident, including the source of the attack, the affected systems, and the actions taken by the attacker. This information is vital for understanding the scope and impact of the incident and for determining the appropriate response. SIEM systems often integrate with other security tools, such as intrusion prevention systems (IPS), firewalls, and endpoint protection solutions, enabling automated responses to certain threats. For example, a SIEM system may automatically block an IP address identified as the source of a DDoS attack or isolate a compromised device from the network to prevent further damage.

One of the challenges of using a SIEM system effectively is managing the volume of data it processes. Large organizations may generate vast amounts of log data from multiple devices and applications, making it difficult to identify relevant information amidst the noise. To address this issue, SIEM systems incorporate filtering and indexing techniques to prioritize the most critical events and reduce the number of false positives. By setting up customized filters and rules, organizations can fine-tune the system to focus on the most significant threats and minimize the impact of irrelevant alerts. Additionally, many SIEM platforms use machine learning and behavioral analytics to improve the accuracy of threat detection, enabling the system to identify new and evolving attack patterns that traditional rule-based methods may miss.

Despite the powerful capabilities of SIEM systems, implementing and maintaining them effectively requires a significant investment of time, effort, and resources. The process of configuring a SIEM system to meet the specific needs of an organization can be complex, as it involves defining security policies, setting up data collection points, and customizing event correlation rules. This requires collaboration between security teams, network administrators, and other IT personnel to ensure that the SIEM system is properly integrated with the organization's existing infrastructure and security controls.

Furthermore, ongoing maintenance is required to keep the system up to date with the latest threat intelligence, software updates, and compliance requirements.

Compliance with regulatory standards is another area where SIEM systems play an essential role. Many industries, such as healthcare, finance, and government, are subject to strict data protection regulations that require organizations to implement specific security measures and maintain detailed logs of system activity. SIEM systems help organizations meet these compliance requirements by providing centralized logging, audit trails, and reports that demonstrate adherence to regulations such as the General Data Protection Regulation (GDPR), the Health Insurance Portability and Accountability Act (HIPAA), and the Payment Card Industry Data Security Standard (PCI DSS). The ability to generate comprehensive reports on security events, user activity, and incident responses simplifies the process of preparing for audits and ensures that organizations can provide the necessary documentation when required.

As organizations continue to face an increasing number of cyber threats, the role of SIEM systems in maintaining security becomes even more critical. The continuous monitoring, event correlation, and incident response capabilities provided by SIEM systems enable organizations to detect and mitigate threats in real time, reducing the impact of potential breaches. Additionally, SIEM systems help improve overall security visibility, allowing organizations to gain a deeper understanding of their network activity and identify vulnerabilities that may have otherwise gone unnoticed. By implementing and maintaining a SIEM system, organizations can strengthen their security posture, enhance their incident response capabilities, and ensure compliance with regulatory standards.

Ultimately, SIEM systems provide a holistic approach to security management by enabling organizations to centralize their security data, improve threat detection and response, and proactively address vulnerabilities. Although configuring and maintaining a SIEM system can be resource-intensive, the benefits it offers in terms of real-time monitoring, correlation, and incident management far outweigh the challenges. As the complexity and frequency of cyberattacks continue to rise, organizations that invest in robust SIEM systems will be better equipped to detect, respond to, and recover from security incidents, thereby safeguarding their critical assets and maintaining the trust of their users.

The Role of Threat Intelligence in Server Security

In today's increasingly connected world, cyber threats continue to evolve in complexity and scale. Servers, being the backbone of most IT infrastructures, are frequent targets for a wide range of malicious activities. From brute-force attacks and ransomware to sophisticated advanced persistent threats (APTs), organizations must be proactive in their approach to security. One of the most effective ways to enhance server security is through the integration of threat intelligence, which provides valuable information that helps organizations identify, understand, and mitigate emerging threats. By leveraging threat intelligence, security teams can gain a deeper understanding of the threat landscape, make more informed decisions, and respond to potential attacks more effectively.

Threat intelligence refers to the collection, analysis, and application of information about existing and potential cyber threats. This information can come from a variety of sources, including open-source intelligence (OSINT), commercial threat intelligence providers, internal security data, and information sharing between organizations. By aggregating and analyzing this data, organizations can gain insights into the tactics, techniques, and procedures (TTPs) used by cybercriminals and threat actors. These insights allow organizations to stay ahead of evolving threats and implement proactive security measures to defend their servers against targeted attacks.

One of the key benefits of threat intelligence in server security is its ability to provide early warning signs of emerging threats. Traditional security measures, such as firewalls and intrusion detection systems (IDS), are reactive by nature. They respond to security events after they occur, often based on known attack patterns or signatures. While these tools are essential for defending servers, they are limited in their ability to detect new and unknown threats. Threat intelligence, on the other hand, provides a proactive layer of defense by alerting security teams to new vulnerabilities, attack methods, and threat actor activities before they have a chance to exploit them. By receiving timely and actionable intelligence, organizations can strengthen their security posture and prevent attacks before they escalate.

Threat intelligence also plays a crucial role in improving incident response and reducing the time it takes to detect and mitigate security incidents. When a server is compromised, quick identification of the attack type, the methods used, and the affected systems is critical for minimizing damage. Threat intelligence feeds can help security teams identify the signs of an attack more quickly by providing real-time data on known threats, attack vectors, and malicious indicators, such as IP addresses, domain names, and malware hashes. This enables organizations to respond rapidly to security breaches, isolate compromised systems, and take appropriate remediation steps. The integration of threat intelligence into incident response processes can significantly reduce response times and improve the overall efficiency of security teams.

Moreover, threat intelligence enhances the ability to prioritize security efforts based on the most relevant and imminent risks. Not all security threats are created equal, and organizations must be able to prioritize their resources and responses effectively. With the help of threat intelligence, security teams can assess the risk level of specific threats and allocate resources to address the most critical vulnerabilities. For example, if a new exploit targeting a widely used server software is identified, threat intelligence can help organizations prioritize patching or mitigating the risk associated with that vulnerability. Similarly, if a particular threat actor is targeting organizations in a specific industry, threat intelligence can help security teams adjust their defense strategies accordingly. By understanding the threat landscape and prioritizing actions based on the latest intelligence, organizations can better allocate their resources and protect their servers against the most pressing risks.

In addition to improving detection and response capabilities, threat intelligence is also essential for strengthening preventive security measures. By analyzing historical threat data, security teams can identify patterns and trends that can inform their security strategy. For example, threat intelligence can reveal common attack vectors and tactics used by cybercriminals to exploit vulnerabilities in server configurations, software, or networks. This information allows organizations to take preventive measures, such as configuring firewalls to block known malicious IP addresses, implementing strict access controls, or hardening server configurations to mitigate specific vulnerabilities. Threat intelligence also helps organizations understand the motivations and goals of threat actors, which can inform the development of more targeted security measures and defenses.

One of the most valuable aspects of threat intelligence is its ability to improve collaboration and information sharing between organizations, industry groups, and governmental bodies. Cyber threats are a global issue, and no organization is completely immune to attacks. By sharing threat intelligence with trusted partners, organizations can benefit from collective knowledge and experience, which can help them better defend their servers against emerging threats. Many government agencies and industry groups, such as the Information Sharing and Analysis Centers (ISACs), provide threat intelligence feeds and resources to help organizations stay informed about the latest risks and vulnerabilities. Additionally, private threat intelligence providers offer commercial services that aggregate and analyze global threat data, providing organizations with actionable insights into current and emerging threats. By participating in information-sharing initiatives and leveraging external threat intelligence, organizations can enhance their ability to detect and defend against cyber threats.

Integrating threat intelligence into server security requires both technical tools and processes. Security Information and Event Management (SIEM) systems, intrusion detection systems (IDS), and endpoint protection platforms can all benefit from the incorporation of threat intelligence feeds. By combining threat intelligence with these security tools, organizations can enhance their detection capabilities, improve event correlation, and streamline incident response. For example, a SIEM system can integrate threat intelligence to correlate external threat data with internal logs and events, helping security teams identify potential threats more effectively. Similarly,

IDS systems can use threat intelligence to detect known attack patterns and malicious activity in real time, providing an additional layer of defense against targeted attacks. Automated threat intelligence platforms can also help security teams streamline the process of collecting, analyzing, and applying intelligence to improve overall server security.

While threat intelligence offers numerous benefits for server security, organizations must also be mindful of the challenges involved in leveraging it effectively. The sheer volume of threat intelligence data can be overwhelming, and it is essential to filter and prioritize the information that is most relevant to the organization's specific needs. Organizations should implement processes for assessing the credibility and reliability of threat intelligence sources to ensure that they are acting on accurate and actionable information. Additionally, threat intelligence must be continuously updated to stay relevant, as the cyber threat landscape is constantly evolving. Organizations should invest in tools and platforms that allow them to ingest, analyze, and act on threat intelligence in real time, ensuring that their server security remains adaptive and resilient.

Incorporating threat intelligence into server security is a powerful approach for staying ahead of the growing array of cyber threats. By providing early warnings, improving detection and response capabilities, and informing preventive measures, threat intelligence strengthens the overall security posture of servers and networks. As cyber threats continue to increase in sophistication, leveraging threat intelligence will remain a crucial element of an effective cybersecurity strategy, helping organizations protect their critical assets and ensure the ongoing security of their server infrastructure.

Hardening Server-based Authentication Services

Authentication services play a crucial role in securing any server, as they act as the gatekeepers that ensure only authorized users can access sensitive systems and data. Server-based authentication services such as LDAP (Lightweight Directory Access Protocol), Kerberos, and RADIUS (Remote Authentication Dial-In User Service) are fundamental to managing user identities and controlling access within enterprise environments. However, these services are often targeted by attackers due to their central role in managing access controls. As such, hardening server-based authentication services is vital to preventing unauthorized access, ensuring the confidentiality of user credentials, and protecting sensitive data from malicious actors.

One of the first steps in hardening authentication services is to ensure that authentication methods are configured with robust, secure protocols. For example, when configuring LDAP, it is crucial to enforce the use of LDAPS (LDAP over SSL/TLS) to ensure that all data transmitted, including user credentials, is encrypted in transit. Without encryption, an attacker could easily intercept sensitive data using man-in-the-middle (MITM) techniques, exposing user credentials and potentially allowing unauthorized access to systems. Similarly, services like RADIUS should also be configured to use secure transport protocols such as IPsec or TLS, ensuring that all communications between the client and the server are encrypted. This reduces the risk of attackers exploiting vulnerabilities in the communication channels and enhances the overall security of the authentication service.

In addition to securing communication channels, the authentication methods themselves must be configured with strong, industry-standard techniques. Password-based authentication, which is still widely used, should be reinforced by enforcing strong password policies. This includes requiring complex passwords, disallowing easily guessable or reused passwords, and ensuring that passwords are stored securely using proper cryptographic hashing algorithms such as bcrypt or PBKDF2. Storing passwords in plain text or using weak hashing algorithms can leave the server vulnerable to attacks like dictionary or brute-force attacks. By enforcing strong password policies and ensuring that passwords are stored securely, the server can significantly reduce the risk of unauthorized access resulting from weak authentication credentials.

In addition to securing passwords, multi-factor authentication (MFA) should be implemented wherever possible. MFA adds an extra layer of security by requiring users to provide more than just a password to authenticate. Typically, MFA involves something the user knows (e.g., a password), something the user has (e.g., a hardware token or smartphone app), or something the user is (e.g., biometric verification). Enabling MFA for authentication services like LDAP and Kerberos can greatly increase the difficulty for attackers attempting to compromise user accounts, as they would need to bypass not only the password but also an additional layer of authentication. For example, MFA can help prevent unauthorized access even if an attacker successfully obtains a user's password through phishing or other means.

Another important aspect of hardening authentication services is controlling access and applying the principle of least privilege. This means that users and administrators should only be granted the minimum level of access necessary to perform their job functions. By minimizing the number of privileged accounts and reducing their permissions, the attack surface is decreased, making it more difficult for attackers to escalate their privileges once they gain access to the server. For example, administrators should not use their privileged accounts for everyday tasks, and access to sensitive systems should be restricted to only those who need it. Additionally, permissions should be reviewed regularly to ensure they remain aligned with the user's role within the organization. This reduces the chances of a compromised account being able to access critical systems or data.

One of the most effective ways to harden authentication services is through regular auditing and monitoring. By continuously tracking authentication attempts and monitoring logs for unusual activity, administrators can detect potential security incidents early and take corrective action before an attack escalates. This includes setting up alerts for failed login attempts, particularly for privileged accounts, as well as monitoring for anomalous behavior such as logins from unusual locations or at unexpected times. Many authentication services, such as Kerberos, provide built-in auditing capabilities that allow administrators to log authentication events, monitor for potential abuse, and identify suspicious activity. By reviewing these logs regularly, administrators can detect signs of malicious activity, such as brute-force attacks or credential stuffing attempts, and respond quickly.

Implementing role-based access control (RBAC) can also improve the security of server-based authentication services. RBAC allows administrators to define roles and assign permissions to those roles rather than to individual users. This makes it easier to manage access control policies and ensures that users are only granted access to the resources they need to perform their jobs. For example, a user in a development role should not have the same level of access as an administrator or a user in a support role. By implementing RBAC and enforcing strict access controls based on roles, organizations can limit the scope of potential damage caused by a compromised account.

In addition to the server configuration and user access controls, the physical security of the server hosting the authentication service should not be overlooked. Authentication servers are critical components of an organization's infrastructure, and compromising them can have devastating consequences. To protect these servers, they should be housed in secure data centers or server rooms with strict physical access controls, such as biometric scanners or keycard access. Furthermore, authentication services should be protected by firewalls, intrusion detection/prevention systems (IDS/IPS), and other network security measures to ensure that only authorized traffic can reach them. This provides an additional layer of defense against remote or physical attacks on the authentication system.

When it comes to authentication protocols like Kerberos, regular key management is essential to ensure the continued security of the system. In Kerberos, tickets and session keys are used to authenticate users and services within the network. These keys should be rotated regularly to reduce the risk of a compromised key being used for unauthorized access. Additionally, administrators should configure Kerberos to use strong encryption algorithms, such as AES-256, to protect the communication between clients and servers. Weak or outdated encryption methods can make the authentication process vulnerable to attacks such as brute-force cracking or key discovery.

Finally, organizations should ensure that their authentication services are always up to date with the latest security patches and updates. Authentication servers, like any other critical infrastructure, can have vulnerabilities that may be exploited by attackers if left unpatched. Regularly applying security patches and keeping the authentication services updated ensures that known vulnerabilities are addressed and that the servers remain protected against emerging threats. Automated patch management tools can help streamline this process, ensuring that updates are applied quickly and consistently across all servers in the environment.

Hardening server-based authentication services is a vital component of an organization's overall security strategy. By implementing robust authentication methods, enforcing the principle of least privilege, applying multi-factor authentication, and ensuring proper access controls, organizations can significantly reduce the risk of unauthorized access to their servers. Regular monitoring, auditing, and vulnerability management further enhance the security posture of authentication services, providing early detection of potential threats and improving incident response capabilities. In an increasingly hostile cybersecurity landscape, the proper hardening of authentication services is essential to safeguarding sensitive data and maintaining the integrity of IT infrastructure.

Securing Serverless Architectures

Serverless architectures are rapidly gaining popularity as organizations look to reduce the complexity of managing traditional server-based infrastructures. In a serverless model, developers can build and deploy applications without having to worry about provisioning and managing servers. Instead, the cloud provider automatically manages the infrastructure, scaling it based on demand and handling the underlying resources. This abstraction offers numerous benefits, including cost efficiency, scalability, and flexibility. However, the security of serverless architectures presents a unique set of challenges that require specialized attention. Since traditional security practices, such as firewalling and access control at the network level, may not be directly applicable in a serverless environment, securing these architectures demands a different approach.

One of the most critical aspects of securing serverless architectures is securing the functions themselves. In a serverless environment, applications are typically broken down into discrete, event-driven functions that run in response to specific triggers, such as an HTTP request or a message in a queue. These functions, often referred to as "serverless functions," run on ephemeral, stateless compute environments. Since these functions can be exposed to the internet or integrated with other services, they can be vulnerable to various types of attacks, such as injection attacks or data exfiltration. To mitigate these risks, developers must ensure that serverless functions are written securely, with a focus on minimizing their attack surface.

One key aspect of securing serverless functions is input validation and sanitization. As with any application, untrusted user input can present a significant security risk if not handled properly. Since serverless functions often handle event data that comes from external sources, it is crucial to validate and sanitize all input before it is processed. For example, if a serverless function is triggered by an HTTP request, it is important to verify that the request data adheres to expected formats and does not contain malicious payloads. Failing to properly validate input can lead to vulnerabilities such as injection attacks, which could allow attackers to execute arbitrary code or access sensitive data.

Another important security consideration is managing the permissions of serverless functions. While serverless architectures abstract away the underlying infrastructure, they still rely on cloud providers' identity and access management (IAM) systems to control access to resources. These permissions define which resources a function can interact with, such as databases, storage systems, or other services. The principle of least privilege should be strictly enforced, ensuring that each serverless function only has the minimum permissions necessary to perform its tasks. For instance, if a function only needs read access to a database, it should not be granted write or delete permissions. Misconfigurations in IAM policies can lead to privilege escalation, allowing attackers to access resources that should be restricted.

In addition to proper permissions management, securing serverless architectures involves ensuring that sensitive data is encrypted both at rest and in transit. Serverless functions often process sensitive data, such as personally identifiable information (PII), financial details, or authentication tokens. To protect this data from unauthorized access, encryption should be used to secure it both during transmission over the network and while stored in databases or other storage systems.

Cloud providers typically offer built-in encryption features for data in transit and at rest, but it is important to ensure that these features are enabled and properly configured for all data handled by serverless functions.

Authentication and authorization are also key concerns when securing serverless architectures. Since serverless functions can be exposed to the internet, they often serve as entry points for external users or systems. Protecting these entry points with proper authentication mechanisms is critical to preventing unauthorized access. For example, using OAuth or API keys to authenticate API requests ensures that only authorized users or systems can trigger the serverless functions. Additionally, implementing token-based authentication, such as JSON Web Tokens (JWT), can help ensure that the requests are valid and have the appropriate level of access.

One of the more unique challenges of securing serverless architectures is ensuring that the underlying cloud infrastructure itself is protected. While cloud providers offer many security features, such as virtual private networks (VPNs), encryption, and intrusion detection systems, organizations must still take responsibility for securing their serverless environments. This includes configuring and managing security settings within the cloud provider's platform and integrating third-party security tools when necessary. Organizations should also be aware of potential misconfigurations or security holes in their serverless architecture, which can result from improper settings or lack of oversight.

Since serverless functions are ephemeral, it is also important to consider their lifecycle and the potential for left-behind resources. For example, if a function is created to interact with a database but is not properly deleted after use, it may remain accessible and vulnerable to attacks. To prevent this, organizations should implement strict policies around the lifecycle management of serverless functions, including automatic deletion of unused resources, monitoring for orphaned resources, and auditing functions to ensure that they do not persist beyond their useful life.

Logging and monitoring are critical components of securing any infrastructure, and serverless architectures are no exception. Since serverless functions are stateless and distributed, tracking their behavior and detecting anomalies can be challenging. To address this, organizations should implement robust logging and monitoring practices to ensure that they can detect and respond to potential security incidents. Most cloud providers offer tools to capture logs from serverless functions, such as AWS CloudWatch or Azure Monitor. These logs can be used to track function execution, monitor for unusual patterns of behavior, and detect potential attacks. Additionally, integrating serverless functions with Security Information and Event Management (SIEM) systems allows security teams to analyze logs and identify threats in real time.

Another critical consideration for serverless security is handling dependencies. Serverless functions often rely on third-party libraries or external services, which can introduce vulnerabilities if not properly managed. For example, a serverless function might use an outdated library with known security flaws, leaving the system vulnerable to attacks. To mitigate this risk, organizations should ensure that their serverless functions are using up-to-date and well-maintained libraries. They should also regularly audit dependencies to ensure that no vulnerabilities are present in the packages used by their serverless functions. Additionally, minimizing the use of external dependencies can reduce the attack surface and make the system more secure.

Finally, testing and securing serverless applications before they are deployed is essential for ensuring their robustness. This includes not only functional testing but also security testing, such as vulnerability assessments and penetration testing. Security testing helps identify potential weaknesses in serverless functions and can reveal misconfigurations, improper access controls, or unaddressed vulnerabilities before an attack occurs. Incorporating security testing into the development lifecycle can help organizations identify and address security issues early, reducing the risk of a successful attack.

Securing serverless architectures requires a combination of best practices that cover a wide range of considerations, from input validation and encryption to access controls and proper function lifecycle management. Since serverless environments introduce unique security challenges, organizations must adapt their security strategies to address these challenges. By implementing strong authentication mechanisms, enforcing the principle of least privilege, ensuring proper lifecycle management, and regularly monitoring and auditing serverless functions, organizations can effectively secure their serverless environments and protect their data from emerging threats.

Continuous Improvement in System Hardening: Staying Ahead of Emerging Threats

System hardening is a critical process in the field of cybersecurity, focused on reducing vulnerabilities and minimizing the attack surface of computing environments. While initial hardening steps are crucial in securing systems, the threat landscape is constantly evolving, requiring organizations to continuously reassess and improve their security measures. Staying ahead of emerging threats is not only about reacting to attacks, but also about being proactive, anticipating future vulnerabilities, and implementing ongoing improvements to systems. This dynamic approach is essential to ensuring that a system remains resilient against evolving cyber threats, particularly as cybercriminals continue to develop more sophisticated techniques and strategies.

The process of system hardening typically involves securing an operating system, applications, and network configurations by eliminating unnecessary services, applying patches, and configuring strong access controls. However, the fundamental challenge is that no security measure is foolproof, and new vulnerabilities can emerge at any time. Hackers and malicious actors are constantly refining their tactics to find new exploits or bypass existing defenses. As a result, a security strategy that is only focused on initial hardening will soon become outdated. Therefore, continuous improvement in system hardening is essential to keeping systems secure in the face of ever-evolving threats.

One of the foundational elements of continuous improvement is regular system patching. Security patches are released frequently by software vendors to address newly discovered vulnerabilities. If patches are not applied promptly, systems become vulnerable to exploitation. Automated patch management tools can help ensure that updates are applied consistently across all systems, reducing the risk of security gaps caused by unpatched vulnerabilities. However, patching alone is not enough. Organizations must be vigilant in tracking emerging threats and understanding the specific patches required to mitigate them. For instance, when a new zero-day vulnerability is discovered, it is important to prioritize the application of patches or workarounds to protect against that particular exploit.

Beyond patching, vulnerability management plays a crucial role in system hardening. Organizations should regularly conduct vulnerability scans to identify potential weaknesses in their systems. Vulnerability scanners help detect outdated software, misconfigured security settings, and other weaknesses that could be exploited by attackers. These tools provide valuable insight into areas of the system that require attention, allowing administrators to take corrective action. However, vulnerability management must be treated as an ongoing process, with scans conducted regularly and results reviewed promptly to ensure vulnerabilities are addressed before they can be exploited.

Access controls are another critical aspect of continuous improvement in system hardening. The principle of least privilege should be enforced at all times, ensuring that users, processes, and systems only have access to the resources necessary for their specific tasks. Over time, access controls should be reevaluated to ensure they remain aligned with the evolving needs of the organization. Employees may change roles, and systems may expand or evolve, making it necessary to adjust permissions accordingly. Regular audits of user access and permission settings should be conducted to identify and remove any unnecessary or excessive access privileges. In addition, multifactor authentication (MFA) should be implemented for all critical systems to ensure that even if credentials are compromised, unauthorized access can still be prevented.

While regular patching and access controls are fundamental to system hardening, addressing security at the application layer is just as important. Applications often introduce vulnerabilities that can be exploited by attackers. Web applications, in particular, are prime targets for cybercriminals. By continuously reviewing and updating the security posture of web applications, organizations can mitigate risks associated with common threats such as SQL injection, cross-site scripting (XSS), and cross-site request forgery (CSRF). Secure coding practices should be enforced throughout the software development lifecycle, with regular security reviews and penetration testing conducted to identify and address vulnerabilities. Continuous monitoring of application behavior also provides insights into potential weaknesses, allowing administrators to respond swiftly to suspicious activities.

Network security is another key area for continuous improvement in system hardening. Firewalls, intrusion detection systems (IDS), and intrusion prevention systems (IPS) form the first line of defense against external threats. However, attackers are constantly evolving their techniques to bypass traditional network security controls. Regularly reviewing and updating firewall rules, IDS/IPS configurations, and network segmentation strategies is necessary to ensure they remain effective in preventing attacks. The adoption of new technologies such as software-defined networking (SDN) and zero-trust architectures can further strengthen network security by dynamically adjusting network traffic flows and restricting access based on user identity and behavior rather than relying solely on traditional perimeter-based defenses.

Furthermore, the growing use of cloud environments presents new challenges for system hardening. Cloud services offer scalability and flexibility, but they also introduce unique risks related to data storage, access control, and service misconfigurations. Continuous improvement in hardening cloud environments requires a focus on cloud-specific security practices, such as securing application programming interfaces (APIs), configuring strong identity and access management (IAM) policies, and ensuring data encryption both at rest and in transit. Cloud providers offer many built-in security tools, but organizations should complement these with their own security measures to ensure comprehensive protection. By continuously monitoring cloud resources and auditing configurations, organizations can detect misconfigurations and potential vulnerabilities that could expose them to attacks.

As the cyber threat landscape evolves, the integration of threat intelligence into system hardening practices has become increasingly important. Threat intelligence provides actionable insights into current and emerging threats, helping organizations stay ahead of attackers. By leveraging threat intelligence feeds and platforms, organizations can gain early warning signs of new vulnerabilities, attack techniques, and threat actor activities. These insights allow security teams to proactively adjust their security measures, such as updating firewall rules, revising patch management processes, and refining detection strategies. Threat intelligence also helps organizations identify patterns of attack that may affect their specific industry or region, enabling them to implement targeted defenses based on the most relevant risks.

Continuous improvement in system hardening also requires a culture of security awareness and training within the organization. Employees are often the weakest link in an organization's security posture, so ensuring that they are well-trained in identifying phishing attacks, practicing good password hygiene, and understanding security policies is essential. Security awareness training should be an ongoing process, with regular updates to address emerging threats. In addition, organizations should foster a culture of security by involving all stakeholders in the hardening process, from developers to network administrators to senior management. Security is not solely the responsibility of the IT department, but rather a collective effort that involves everyone in the organization.

Lastly, regular testing and simulation of attack scenarios, such as penetration testing and red teaming, help organizations evaluate the effectiveness of their security measures and identify gaps that need to be addressed. These tests simulate real-world attacks and provide valuable feedback on how well systems would respond to actual threats. By continuously testing and refining their defenses, organizations can identify weaknesses before attackers do and make necessary improvements to strengthen their security posture.

Continuous improvement in system hardening is essential for staying ahead of the rapidly evolving cyber threat landscape. As new vulnerabilities emerge and attackers refine their tactics, organizations must continuously reassess and enhance their security measures to ensure the resilience of their systems. By maintaining a proactive approach to patching, access control, application security, network defense, and threat intelligence, organizations can build a security posture that evolves alongside the threats they face. In this dynamic environment, the key to long-term success in system hardening is adaptability and vigilance, ensuring that defenses are always one step ahead of potential attackers.